our account

a History of BB&T

About the Cover

Left – In 1903 Branch Banking built this neo-classical structure in Wilson, N.C., as its headquarters. It was the first structure in Wilson County placed on the National Register of Places. In 2012, the building housed the Wilson Arts Council.

Top, right – BB&T's corporate headquarters building in Winston-Salem, N.C.

Bottom, right – Bryan Larsen's "Our Best Days are Ahead" painting, which was used on the cover of the 2008 BB&T Annual Review, was the inspiration for this BB&T "Lighthouse" painting. Created in 2009, Larsen's "Lighthouse" painting symbolized the strength, stability and dependable beacon of light BB&T Corporation portrayed during the height of the recession.

First Edition
1962

Sixth Edition
1990

Second Edition
1963

Seventh Edition
1991

Third Edition
1979

Eighth Edition
1992

Fourth Edition
1986

Ninth Edition
1999

Fifth Edition
1988

Tenth Edition
2012

Acknowledgments

Thanks to all those who helped make this tenth edition of the BB&T History Book possible. Capturing the past several years of BB&T's history would not have been possible without the countless individuals who shared memories, photos, facts and figures as well as assisted in fact-checking, proofreading and more. Special thanks to J. Moore Bannister for coordinating and conducting interviews and research; Sharon Berry for conducting interviews and research and capturing it in writing; and Jennifer Reardon for creating the design and layout of "Our Account: A History of BB&T."

Table of Contents

Chapter	Page

Chapter	Page

BB&T Mission

To make the world a better place to live by:

Helping our **clients** achieve economic success
and financial security;

Creating a place where our **employees** can learn,
grow and be fulfilled in their work;

Making the **communities** in which we work
better places to be; and thereby:

Optimizing the long-term return to our **shareholders**, while
providing a safe and sound investment.

Foreword

In any aspect of life it's helpful to know your heritage, whether it's your family, your country, your faith, your employer or your bank.

We believe it's important to show respect for our forefathers but also to understand and learn from the challenges they faced. Our heritage provides vital information about the practices and beliefs that served our forefathers well and can help us achieve similar success. And, hopefully, we learn from any mistakes they made so we won't repeat them.

BB&T's past trials, tribulations and successes have certainly helped build and mold the values and principles that have made this one of the most sound and secure financial institutions in the country today.

History also gives us hope. The BB&T legacy began in 1872 during some of the most difficult times our country has ever faced. We survived the Great Depression and beat the odds of growing from a small North Carolina bank to becoming one of the largest in the country. Now we're emerging from the Great Recession stronger than ever. This gives us hope for the future and the contributions we can make for the good of our fellow man.

BB&T carved its vision, mission and values out of this rich history. They're not just empty words on a dusty old plaque. They're the cornerstones of who we were yesterday and who we are today. And, they will guide us as we become the BB&T of tomorrow.

Kelly S. King

Kelly King

Chairman and Chief Executive Officer

History, by apprising the people of the past,

will enable them to judge of the future;

it will avail them of the experience of other times

and other nations; it will qualify them

as judges of the actions and designs of men...

Thomas Jefferson

Introduction

The new millennium ushered in unimaginable challenges and opportunities for BB&T and the entire financial services industry. These events included new leadership, rapid technological advancements, new and expanding markets, and widespread regulatory changes as the United States faced the most difficult economic environment since the Great Depression.

Through it all, BB&T's Executive Management maintained that BB&T's vision, mission, values and client-driven strategy as a constant.

A NEW ERA

King

During the first decade, BB&T executed its succession plan, culminating with the longtime Chairman and Chief Executive Officer John Allison passing the baton to Kelly King. King took the helm in 2009 with a relatively new Executive Management team, following the retirements of Allison, Chief Financial Officer Scott Reed, Chief Credit Officer Ken Chalk and Chief Operating Officer Henry Williamson.

Joining King, Manager of Administrative Services Rob Greene and Operations Division Manager Leon Wilson on the Executive Management team over time were President of Community Banking Ricky Brown, Chief Financial Officer Daryl Bible, Enterprise Risk Manager Barbara Duck, Deposit Services Manager Donna Goodrich, Chief Operating Officer Chris Henson, Chief Risk Officer Clarke Starnes and Chief Marketing Officer Steve Wiggs.

The carefully orchestrated succession plan, positioned BB&T well to face a new and unforeseen frontier. The new Executive Management team provided the direction needed for BB&T to respond swiftly to technological changes, new regulatory requirements, shaken consumer confidence and the acquisition of Montgomery, Ala.-based Colonial Bank in 2009, the largest acquisition in the company's history.

Colonial was one of many financial institutions to fail as the U.S. economy unraveled. In an FDIC-assisted deal, BB&T acquired $20 billion in deposits and $22 billion in assets, without the credit risk or problem loans, and become the eighth largest bank in the nation based on deposits. BB&T's market share in Alabama and Florida, two key markets in the Southeast, climbed to No. 4 and No. 5 respectively. Colonial also gave BB&T its first banking presence in Texas. *Time* magazine ranked the Colonial acquisition No. 3 on its list of Top 10 Best Business Deals for 2009.

Colonial was one of many financial services companies affected by the national banking crisis resulting in the Great Recession. Beginning in 2008, prestigious financial services companies made shocking announcements almost daily about their struggles or failures as a result of diversified income strains. BB&T Insurance, Wealth and Lending contributed significantly to BB&T's earnings as the bank faced an array of challenges from loan defaults and reduced fee revenues. Executive Management and all BB&T employees worked feverishly to prepare for and address client concerns about banks' safety and soundness while simultaneously addressing regulatory requirements, resulting in product and service changes, and an increased emphasis on efficiency. Although Colonial was the largest acquisition in recent years, it followed two other major deals – the One Valley merger in 2000 and First Virginia in 2003.

Advancements in technology enabled numerous enhancements to BB&T's automated delivery channels. With dramatically increasing numbers of online clients, BB&T created a new eBusiness department to ensure the bank's online products and services met client expectations and clients could access them all with a single login. In 2008, BB&T introduced mobile alerts so clients could send and receive account information through cell phone text messaging. Monitoring accounts and making transactions by phone became even easier for clients in 2010 when BB&T released its first smartphone application.

In the Community Bank, BB&T formally dedicated a sales force to its BB&T@Work program, which encourages employees of participating companies to bank with BB&T by providing them with exclusive discounts and benefits on a variety of BB&T financial products and services. In 2011,

BB&T@Work accounted for 26 percent of new retail transaction accounts opened each month and touted 60,000 company partners throughout the bank's footprint.

Due to inflated costs of bank acquisitions in the mid-2000s, BB&T turned its attention to organic growth. One strategy was sports marketing. In 2006, BB&T announced its first NASCAR sponsorship, a partnership with Richard Childress Racing. A Six Sigma project revealed that the investment paid for itself with the business gained by client entertainment and other business development activities. The sponsorship also gave BB&T an estimated television advertising value of $6.5 million in 2007.

In 2009, King recognized the need for more hands-on community involvement and launched The Lighthouse Project as a way to shine a beacon of light into a world that for some seemed dark and hopeless. BB&T employees worked to help the many overwhelmed and underfunded nonprofit organizations during business hours through volunteer service and corporate financial support. As employees reached out to help others, they reported personally benefitting as much or more from the service initiative as those they sought to help. Employees voted in 2011 to repeat the Lighthouse Project for a fourth year in 2012.

King adopted "Our Best Days are Ahead" as his mantra – not to imply a more prosperous time in the near future, but to encourage employees to do their best and strive to make a positive, meaningful impact on the lives of others.

"We interact with untold numbers of clients, families and communities," King said. "In these economic times we have an enormous opportunity to have a positive impact on these individuals and help them achieve their life's dreams, goals and hopes. That's the real point." ∎

BB&T Corporate Headquarters in Winston-Salem, N.C.

CHAPTER II

A Survivor

Alpheus Branch and Thomas Jefferson Hadley founded the organizational ancestor of BB&T in the wake of the Civil War. BB&T survived all of the panics and wars that followed. Even during the depression years of the 1930s when banks throughout the country were closing their doors, and strong institutions were finding weaknesses in their foundations, BB&T never refused a withdrawal or failed to issue dividends on its stock to its owners.

THE WORLD OF BRANCH AND HADLEY

When hostilities ended in 1865 and the South was forced to accept defeat, the farmers-turned-soldiers returned home and found their property destroyed, livestock gone, tools and equipment either ruined or lost and their money worthless. The world that they had left their homes to defend existed no longer. The world to which they returned was chaotic and was to remain so for several years.

Historian R. D. W. Connor[*] wrote about the war's aftermath:

> … *it was indeed a heart-breaking time, amid the wreck – no government, no law, no money. The property of many, especially of orphans, held by fiduciaries, invested in State and Confederate securities, gone, and the widows and orphans with no man to provide. Only paper money had been current, and that was without value. There was no currency. All that was left was the home, the family ties, the hands, the heart of the individual. There were no organized industries, no capital, no work to be done, save plowing the fields; other than that, the ordinary occupation of civilized man ceased. Provisions were scarce, and in those zones where the army had been the people had none.*[1]

---

[*]R. D. W. Connor, first archivist of the United States, was son of H.G. Connor, a president of Branch Banking Company.

When the war debts in North Carolina were repudiated, the banks were wrecked, as were private fortunes. Thousands were reduced to extreme poverty, business came to a halt, and every bank in North Carolina was liquidated.[2] The historian Samuel A'Court Ashe comments:

> The old State banks were no more; Congress had virtually forbidden State banks by imposing a heavy tax on their issue and it had so limited the number of National banks that in 1867 only ten new banks could be established in the entire Union, and in the following years, respectively, only 12, 9 and 22, and of these the North got the lion's share. So only two or three banks were in that period allowed in North Carolina. The State was virtually denied banking facilities, as were all the other Southern States.[3]

Though many banks were chartered from the period 1865 to 1870, only a small percentage was able to organize because the necessary capital could not be raised.[4] Money was scarce and those who did have some preferred other types of investment.[5]

The war was devastating enough, but events afterward compounded the injury. Congress imposed a tax on cotton, which drew much money out of the state, but the tax that the North Carolina General Assembly put on land (practically the state's only asset) produced even more dire results. The value of farm land in North Carolina had dropped from $143,301,065 in 1860 to $78,211,083 in 1870.[6]

The period between 1865 and 1870 was fraught with corruption in government. For example, taxable property in 1860 was assessed at $292,000,000 and the amount of taxes collected was only $543,000. In 1870, when the assessed property had dropped to $130,000,000 the state collected $1,160,000 in taxes.[7] The old state debt, exclusive of war debts, was approximately $16,000,000 and the legislature of 1868 increased it by $13,315,000, though no railroads were laid, no public schools constructed and no public buildings built.[8] It was indeed a time of "extravagance, bribery, corruption, oppression… and lawlessness."[9]

In the next few years, conditions changed little. One historian says that in 1875, "The plundered people only knew that out of $16,000,000 voted by the Legislature for 'public works of improvement,' but $500,000 had ever been devoted to that purpose."[10]

Thus, the state faced a broken economy with corruption in government, and when help seemed to come from no quarter, North Carolinians turned to each other for aid.

CREDIT AND THE PRIVATE BANKER

The only practical basis on which business could be conducted was credit. A more fortunate neighbor advanced money, or a merchant extended credit secured by a lien on unplanted crops. Cotton was the money crop in Eastern North Carolina during this period, so "… this crop-lien system helped to perpetuate the one-crop system because the merchant based his loans upon the amount of land to be planted in cotton … "[11]

In addition to all of his other problems, the farmer in North Carolina had nature to cope with; crops in the period following 1865 were not good. Agriculture in North Carolina from 1865 until the turn of the century "fell on evil days… The price of cotton fell from a dollar a pound in 1865 to twenty-five cents a pound in the seventies.*… "[12]

Since Congress had succeeded in virtually denying the Southern states any banking facilities whatsoever, most of the banking in North Carolina, particularly in small towns, was carried on by private institutions. "Many of them operated for only a short time; a number were operated in conjunction with other businesses and never amounted to much as banking institutions; while a small number were either successful as private institutions or were forerunners of important chartered banks. One of these was Branch and Hadley, opened in 1872 in Wilson."[13]

It is almost impossible to imagine how farmers and businessmen would have conducted business without the aid of private bankers during this period.

As has been noted, many banks were chartered during the period from 1865 to 1872, but lack of funds prevented them from organizing. Some that did organize survived only a year or two. Tables I, II and III list those that were organized between 1865 and 1872 and that lasted at least as long as 1872.

*The price dropped to nine cents in the eighties and to five cents in the nineties.

TABLE I[14]
North Carolina Private Banks
Established Between 1865 and 1872

Name and Location	Dates of Operation	Remarks
E. Sluder Asheville	1865-1891	Became Sluder and Barnard in 1884.
Wilson and Shober Greensboro	1868-1878	
Rountree and Webb New Bern	1870-1881	Became R. H. Rountree & Co. in 1875.
Guirkin and Company Elizabeth City	1871-1898	
D. A. Davis Salisbury	1872-1924	(Became Davis & Wiley Bank in 1882.) Incorporated in 1889. Operated under numerous names, underwent several mergers.
Branch and Hadley	1872-present	Changed name in 1887 to Branch and Company, Bankers, and to Branch Banking Company in 1900, operating under the charter granted in 1889.

TABLE II[14]
North Carolina State Banks
Established Between 1865 and 1872

Name and Location	Dates of Operation	Remarks
Bank of Greensboro Greensboro	1869-1923	Became National Bank of Greensboro in 1876.
Bank of Mecklenburg Charlotte	1870-1875	
Bank of Statesville Statesville	1870-1876	
The Dawson Bank Wilmington	1872-1877	
Bank of New Hanover* Wilmington	1872-1893	
Warren Savings Bank Warrenton	1872-1882	

* Also operated branches at Wadesboro and Goldsboro.

TABLE III[14]
North Carolina National Banks
Established Between 1865 and 1872

Name and Location	Dates of Operation	Remarks
First National Bank Charlotte	1865-1930	
Raleigh National Bank of North Carolina Raleigh	1865-1885	
First National Bank Wilmington	1866-1891	
First National Bank Salem	1866-1879	
National Bank New Bern	1866-1929	
State National Bank Raleigh	1868-1888	
Citizens National Bank Raleigh	1870-1930	
Peoples National Bank Fayetteville	1871-1891	
Fayetteville National Bank Fayetteville	1871-1905	(Became a state bank in 1887.) As Bank of Fayetteville, it merged in 1905 with Fourth National Bank of Fayetteville which closed in 1916.
Merchants & Farmers' National Bank Charlotte	1872-1934	

CHAPTER III

Branch and Hadley

*Alpheus Branch and Thomas Jefferson Hadley were both prominent
and well thought of in the Wilson community, and therefore it was only
natural that they would join forces in 1872 and form a company that was
sorely needed at that time. They called the new business Branch
and Hadley, forerunner to today's multi-billion dollar company, BB&T
Corporation.*

The town of Wilson was only 23 years old and had grown from 89
residents in 1849 (the year of incorporation) to a population of 1,036 in
1870.[1] It was gradually becoming the trading center for the surrounding
agricultural area.*

*In addition to other activities, Branch and Hadley accepted time deposits,
sold foreign drafts and engaged in the usual transactions of the private
banker. This business was located at the corner of Barnes and Tarboro
streets and was known briefly as Branch, Hadley and Farmer.** (See 1882
map on page 32.)*

*The partnership between Mr. Branch and Mr. Hadley continued until 1887
when " ... Branch bought Hadley's interest and the bank became known as
'Branch and Company, Bankers.' "[2] This same year the company moved to
a location on Nash Street two doors west of the Downtown Office, which
was the home office from 1903 until 1971.*

---

* By contrast, Bath, North Carolina's oldest town, was already 168 years old.
It had been established in 1704.
** Charles Farmer, bookkeeper, did not remain with the firm very long.

ALPHEUS BRANCH

Alpheus Branch, for whom the bank is named, was born in Halifax County on May 7, 1843. His father, Captain S. Warren Branch, was an extensive planter and sent his son to be educated at Deems Military Academy in Wilson, Horner School at Oxford and Trinity College. Alpheus left Trinity at the age of 17 to volunteer in the Scotland Neck Cavalry, in which he served with gallantry.[3]

After his discharge from the Confederate Army, he returned to Halifax and became successful enough during the three years following 1865 to become private banker for neighboring farmers. He received deposits from them, put the money to use and paid them interest until the funds were withdrawn to finance spring planting.[4]

In 1865, Mr. Branch married Nannie Barnes, daughter of General Joshua Barnes, one of Wilson's founders. They moved to Wilson, and by 1869 Mr. Branch had established a mercantile business called Branch and Company.[5]

Throughout his relatively short life, Mr. Branch was destined to be a successful businessman. He engaged in many business enterprises, such as Wilson Cotton Mills (established in 1883), of which he was president and principal owner. He was a director of the Wilmington and Weldon Railroad and owned a considerable amount of its stock.[6] He was one of the original directors of the Bank of Wilson (later the First National Bank of Wilson), chartered in 1874.[7]

Mr. Branch was a member of the Episcopal Church, but he did not limit his charities to that denomination. Every account of his life underscores his philanthropies as well as his attention to the civic affairs in Wilson. He was conservative in his business practices, and his will attests his concern for his fellow man. In it he made his estate liable for all of the obligations of the bank.

Mr. Branch has been described by his grandson, F. L. Carr, as a small, extremely dignified man who always wore a Prince Albert coat and a top hat.

THOMAS JEFFERSON HADLEY

Thomas Jefferson Hadley was born on July 9, 1838, in Wayne County in a section that is now Wilson County. He was educated at the Wilson Male Academy and the University of North Carolina, where he received bachelor of arts and law degrees. When the War Between the States broke out, he enlisted as a private and emerged as a captain.

Mr. Hadley was head of the movement in Wilson to establish and organize the first system of public schools and became the first chairman of the board of trustees. His own early training had been acquired at the inadequate schools of the day, and he never lost sight of the need for public education.

An account of the time states: "In person Mr. Hadley is pleasant and easy in manner without compromising his natural dignity."[8] After a long and useful life, Mr. Hadley died on August 3, 1917.

THE PANIC OF 1873

While the South struggled, the East, North and West had prospered since the war, and many new industries flourished, especially the building of railroads. Between 1865 and 1873, 30,000 miles of rail were laid, though only a small percentage in North Carolina.[9] In 1873, an economic panic resulted from the mismanagement of banks by state governmental authorities. Though the country's economy was disrupted, the panic did not affect North Carolina as greatly as other sections of the country because the state was still recovering from reconstruction days.[10]

There is no evidence that Branch and Hadley suffered as a direct result of the panic, though undoubtedly the panic delayed the recovery of the South's still unhealthy economy.

On November 25, 1873, the State of North Carolina had funds deposited in Wilson in the amount of $10,724.30.[11] Since Branch and Hadley was the only bank known to be located in Wilson at that time, it is apparent that these funds were deposited with them.

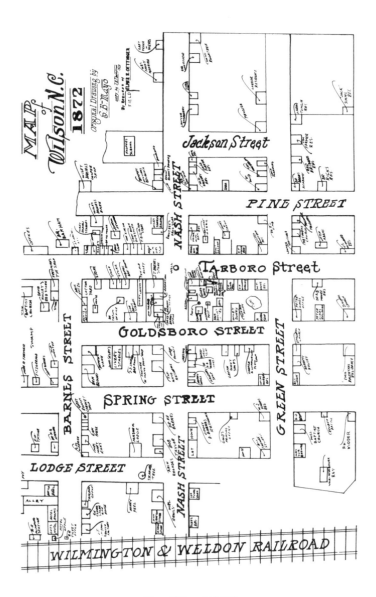

Map of Wilson, NC, 1872.

WILSON IN THE 1880s

In the 1880s, Wilson was described by a local paper as "beautiful, healthful, and thriving."[12] Josephus Daniels says, "In the early eighties Wilson was strictly a cotton town. Aside from two carriage factories, one foundry, a plow factory and a cotton mill, there were no industrial plants. People depended almost solely on cotton … "[13] Mr. Daniels, publisher of the *Wilson Advance*, goes on to relate:

> *It was not until 1884 that Wilson farmers thought their lands were suitable for growing the bright tobacco which is the main ingredient of cigarettes. Up to that time the only tobacco raised in Wilson was that of some farmers who grew a few stalks in fence corners for their own use. In 1884 several farmers decided they would experiment with raising tobacco. When it was cured and sold on the Henderson market, they received four times as much for tobacco grown on an acre as they netted on cotton. They came to the Advance office and showed some of the tobacco like that they had sold and gave the figure of the prices received. I published an interview with them and printed their experience.[14]*

Mr. Daniels said that he advised farmers to grow a few acres of tobacco, but some of Wilson's citizens disagreed with him. He quotes Thomas J. Hadley as saying:

> *It is a dangerous experiment. Tobacco is a gambler's crop. It exhausts the land. Now cotton is a crop you can depend on. Our land is suited to its growth … Let the Piedmont people raise the speculative tobacco crop and let Eastern North Carolina stick to the crop for which its land and labor are adapted.[15]*

BRANCH AND COMPANY, BANKERS

In 1887 Mr. Branch bought Mr. Hadley's interest in Branch and Hadley for which he gave him a check for $81,000. This is said to be the largest check to have been written in Wilson County up to that time. At this time the name was changed to Branch and Company, Bankers, and the company moved to a location on Nash Street.

* Erroneously written "Breston" in the original charter.

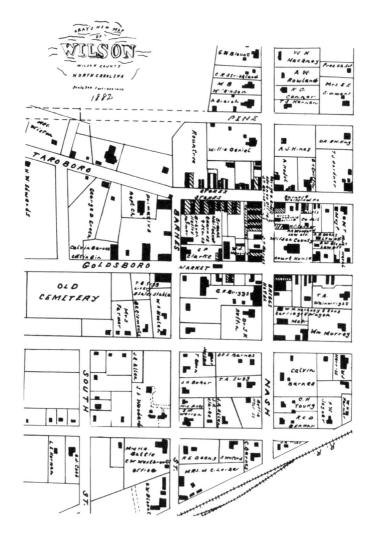

Wilson in 1882. Branch, Hadley and Farmer is located at the corner of Barnes and Tarboro streets, and Mr. Branch's home is at the corner of Pine and Nash.

THE CHARTER OF 1889

In 1889, Mr. Branch, together with T. J. Hadley, General Joshua Barnes, J. F. Bruton,* R. L. Thompson and Walter Brodie, secured a charter from the legislature of North Carolina for the Wilson Banking and Trust Company. At the 1891 session of the legislature the name was changed to The State Bank of Wilson, and in 1893 it was changed again to The Branch Banking Company.[16]

Herbert Hall Mitchell writes, "Many private banks were opened between 1871 and 1899. Some of these institutions operated for a number of years without a charter but most of them either closed or converted to state or national institutions within a short time … Some banks continued to operate as private institutions for a number of years after their charters were received. A notable example of this was the Branch Banking Company of Wilson which received a charter from the state in 1889 but operated as a private institution until 1900."[17]

WILSON IN THE 1890s

The tobacco market opened in Wilson in 1890 and had an immediate effect on the town. The Wilson Mirror tells of hordes of strangers pouring into town and an editorial welcomed them to prosperous, beautiful Wilson, and encouraged them to stay and plant the "lands just now found out to be most admirably adapted to the cultivation of tobacco … "[18]

That year saw the sale of 50,000 pounds of tobacco, followed by 2,000,000 the next year, and 3,000,000 in 1892.[19]* That year Wilson acquired electric street lights and its first water main, and the population of Wilson jumped from 2,126[20] in 1890 to 3,525[21] in 1900.

THE DEATH OF ALPHEUS BRANCH

Alpheus Branch died on January 3, 1893, and in his will he appointed William Preston Simpson and Henry Groves Connor co-executors of his estate. He directed that his estate be liable for the debts of the bank:

* In 1987 the Wilson market sold approximately 62,700,000 pounds of tobacco.

I wish and direct my Executor, W. P. Simpson, immediately upon my death to take charge and control of the banking business of Branch & Co. in the town of Wilson, N. C. and continue without interruption the said business, so long as in his opinion, it will promote the interest of the depositors and of my said Estate. I hereby empower the said W. P. Simpson, as my said Executor, to do any and all acts, which may be necessary to the Execution of the provisions of this clause of my will and I hereby expressly charge my Estate with liability for any and all acts done or performed and all obligations contracted by him in the Execution of this trust in respect to the said banking business. The said W. P. Simpson shall when in his judgment it will promote the interest of depositors, creditors of said bank and of my Estate, proceed to close and settle up the said banking business and pay over and account to my Estate for the proceeds thereof. I wish my said Executor W. P. Simpson to consult with his Co-Executor in regard to all questions of a legal character arising in the management of said banking business.[22]

Thus, W. P. Simpson became president of the bank during what was to become another panic year.

"A GENTLEMAN OF BRAWNY BRAIN"

The year 1893 was a panic year and though over 400 banks[23] throughout the country failed, only one in North Carolina did so.[24] Business, however, was affected, and it was not until 1898 that the state fully recovered.[25]

A few days after the death of Mr. Branch, the *Wilson Mirror* published the following article:

The banking business of Branch & Co., Bankers, will be carried on as heretofore, and will not be disturbed in the least by the death of the lamented Mr. Al Branch, who established and conducted it so successfully. The well equipped and admirably poised W. P. Simpson, a gentleman of brawny brain and excellent judgment and penetrating ken and fine discriminating powers, will take the desk made vacant by the death of Mr. Branch, and exercise a general supervision over the entire business, while the

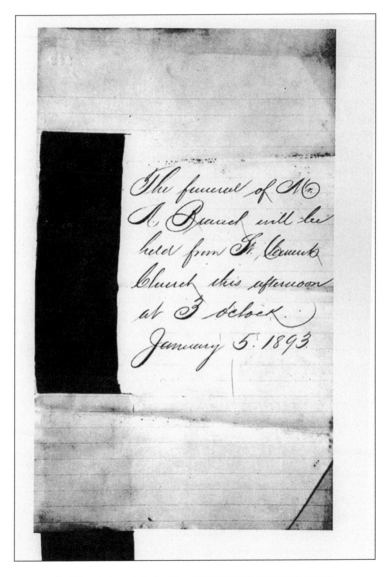

Invitations to funerals during this period often had a yard or two of wide,
black ribbon attached, which could be cut into arm bands.

*efficient and able and very correct cashier J. C. Hales will render
most valuable assistance. Mr. Simpson is not only the willingly
acknowledged best accountant in the State, but he is an affable,
approachable, sympathetic, most polished gentleman, and while
he had that firmness and decision of purpose, which will make
him protect the interests of the business, yet, at the same time, he
had that "suaviter in modo" and delightfulness of bearing which
makes any transaction with him most agreeable and pleasant. In
this connection we will state that the Bank is in a good, strong,
healthy, vigorous condition, and that its strength or reliability
will not be in the least weakened or impaired by the death of the
able founder.*[26]

Mr. Simpson's three years as president were not easy ones. The tobacco
market, which ultimately was to bring fame and fortune to Wilson, caused
him a great deal of difficulty, and in 1895 he wrote to a fellow banker, "Of all
the different and various kinds of business we have engaged in, the tobacco
business is the least satisfactory."[27]

Upon Mr. Simpson's death on June 3, 1896, Judge H. G. Connor took over
the management of Branch and Company, Bankers, and remained president
until 1900 when the company was bought by Branch Banking Company. He
was elected president of this company and remained so until 1907.

H. G. CONNOR, President.   J. C. HALES, Cashier.

BRANCH & CO.,--BANKERS.

Paid up Capital   -   -   -   **$ 50.000.**
Surplus   -   -   -   -   -   **7.000.**

Will take pleasure in extending all possible accommodation to customers,
consistent with sound business principles and safe banking.

Advertisement in the Wilson Times, September 4, 1896.

Advertisement in the Wilson Times, December 20, 1912.

NORTH CAROLINA BANKERS ASSOCIATION

Cashier J. C. Hales attended the organizational meeting of the North Carolina Bankers Association in 1897 at Morehead City. Thomas H. Battle of Rocky Mount was elected president.[28] Mr. Battle had been interested in forming an association since 1892, and he wrote in that year of the necessity of such an organization, also giving an insight into the economic condition of the country:

> ... the formation of personal acquaintance with each other, the making more uniform our business methods, the giving opportunity for intelligent discussion are some of the results.

> Some of us, too, would like to hear a discussion of the financial needs of the country. Something is clearly wrong in a system that allows the rich reserve city banks (without authority except the expediency of the case) to protect themselves by the issue of unlimited paper money in the shape of clearinghouse certificates, whenever occasion requires it; but gives our smaller banks in poorer sections no elasticity whatever, nor even any collateral support from each other.[29] ∎

Bank of Lumberton Opens

Not long after Mr. Simpson's death, a handful of men in a small rural town 90 miles southwest of Wilson pooled fifteen thousand dollars to launch a business that would become the predecessor of Southern National Bank. Residents of Lumberton, N.C., and Robeson County had tired of traveling to Wilmington to do their banking. Though that outlay is minuscule by today's billion-dollar standards, it was hard to come by in 1897, just thirty-two years after the War Between the States ransacked the Southern economy. Raising that kind of capital required an audacious entrepreneur with the ability to find other investors who could be convinced to invest in risky ventures such as starting a bank.

Such a man was Angus Wilton McLean.

ANGUS MCLEAN

McLean faced one self-imposed obstacle in launching his bank. At 27, and only a few years out of law school at the University of North Carolina, he felt he was too young to command the respect needed to interest financial backers. Compared to the older businessmen he knew, many of whom were battle-hardened Confederate Army veterans, he was still wet behind the ears. He decided an older, more established man should be the first president of the Bank of Lumberton.

The solution was in his own law firm. Thomas McNeill was in his fifties, a former legislator, a respected lawyer, a Confederate veteran and a large landowner. McNeill would make a perfect president. With McNeill on record as president, McLean secured investors and a board of directors drawn from prominent men of the region. McNeill, McLean, R. D. Caldwell, C. B. Townsend and S. A. Edmund were all from Lumberton. R. L. Steele, W. L. F. Steele and T. C. Guthrie were from Rockingham, a town about 50 miles away. H. B. Jennings of Bennettsville, South Carolina, rounded out the

Angus Wilton McLean, shown here early in his illustrious career, did not think of himself as a banker, politician or lawyer. He preferred to be thought of as a business builder.

original board. McNeill was named president, Caldwell vice president, and Townsend was appointed cashier, the bank's first employee, a position comparable to today's branch manager.

The local newspaper, *The Robesonian*, praised the coming of the institution the month before the bank opened:

> *It is probably not amiss to say in this connection that the new enterprise had no more zealous friend than Mr. A. W. McLean. He has been at work upon it and agitating the question for the past two years. The charter was drawn by him and his personal efforts were a large factor in having the two sessions of the Legislature act upon it. But for his recent active work it is probable that the organization would not have been perfected so soon.*

The bank was off to a good beginning to do just that when the first major change in the bank's management structure was made. Barely a year and a half after its founding, Thomas McNeill was appointed judge of Superior Court. He could not keep both offices, so he was forced to resign as president on December 21, 1898. The unanimous choice to take his place was Angus Wilton McLean, age 28.

BANKING ONLY ONE OF MCLEAN'S GOALS

Perhaps one of the more amazing facets of McLean's illustrious career is that he likely never counted the creation of the bank among his greatest accomplishments. It was simply one of the goals he set for himself, the industrious Scotsman making the most of his time. McLean also conducted a law practice, founded a railroad, started a land development company, created a trust company and built three cotton mills. Nonetheless, Mr. McLean's persistence led to the founding of the Bank of Lumberton in 1897, the forerunner to Southern National Bank.

He found time to act as North Carolina Democratic Party chairman, attend several U.S. presidential nominating conventions, act as Undersecretary of the U.S. Treasury and serve as chairman of the War Finance Commission in World War I. When he returned home from Washington, he ran for and won the election as North Carolina's Governor. While in Raleigh, his conservative Scottish financial background rose to the top again, leading him to pass landmark legislation that brought the state's budget under executive control.

That led to the common practice today of North Carolina governors submitting balanced budgets to the legislatures.

COMMITTED TO LUMBERTON CUSTOMERS

Though all these interests competed for his time, he still kept his commitments to Bank of Lumberton customers. Even while living in Washington, McLean made sure bank customers were served. Every Thursday night, he reserved a sleeping berth aboard a southbound train. Arriving in Fayetteville at dawn on Fridays, he would catch a ride to Lumberton and go directly to the bank's office before even going to his home two blocks away. He would meet with the bank's major customers Friday, spend Saturdays going over the books, Sunday mornings in church and Sunday nights on a train bound for Washington.

McLean did not think of himself as a banker, a lawyer or even a governor. He was a business builder. That was one of his goals in life, to start companies that would prosper, provide a return on investment for their owners, create jobs for their employees and expand the tax base that would benefit his city, county and state.

Not coincidentally, those were the same goals that drove the Bank of Lumberton, which changed its name to Southern National Bank in 1959. The bank was first successful servicing the small farmers surrounding its base of operations. By 1955, Hector MacLean, the youngest son of Wilton McLean who preferred the Scottish spelling of the family name, was named president and led the bank through unprecedented growth over the next 35 years. With Hector MacLean at the helm, the bank began to aggressively expand to other small towns "Down East." By the 1970s, it was moving into the larger cities of North Carolina, and by the 1980s it was moving into South Carolina.

IMAGE GONE AS SMALL-TOWN BANK

The bank started the 1990s off with two major announcements. Hector MacLean, who built Southern National into a statewide, multi-billion-dollar financial institution, retired as chairman of the board. During his 35 years as leader of the bank, assets had grown from $11 million to more than $3.3 billion. Deposits had grown from $10 million to more than $2.2 billion. The number of branches had increased to 148 branches spread over two states.

MacLean's successor as corporate chairman was Glenn Orr, who would later orchestrate with BB&T Chairman John Allison what some investors and analysts would describe as the most effective merger-of-equals in the banking industry's history. By 1995, Southern National Bank had completely shed its image as a small-town bank. In less than four decades, it had gone from a single office to more than 230 branches in 118 cities. It had established itself as an innovative financial institution ready to pioneer new products, try new forms of advertising and reshape traditional banking services into forms its customers readily accepted. ■

Hector MacLean, near the end of his active career with the bank, took a moment to pose by a painting of his father's mansion, which was demolished as a site for the bank's headquarters in Lumberton, N.C.

CHAPTER IV

The Early Years of the Bank of Lumberton

The early years of the Bank of Lumberton passed easily with few problems. Founding director T. C. Guthrie, a Rockingham attorney, resigned within a year, transferring his ten shares to the Steele family. He sent a letter of regret to the other board members, noting: "My selling out was from no dissatisfaction with the investment and no disbelief in the prospects of success for the bank, but just because I preferred to have the money."

By 1899, the cost-conscious board noted with a little irritation that the first year's expenses of running the bank had totaled $2,799. The second year's expenses had jumped to $2,849. They asked the president to investigate ways of holding down costs.

Even considering the higher expenses, the bank was a money-maker. In 1900, the board recommended paying a 3 percent dividend and voted a twenty-five dollar bonus to President McLean in appreciation for his services. This bonus was on top of McLean's annual salary of forty dollars per year.

By 1901, many of the original directors moved on. A. E. White, a Lumberton merchant and businessman, joined the board. By 1904, the capital stock had increased to fifty thousand dollars.

"THE PANIC OF 1907"

The county's farmers were flocking to the bank. In January 1905, its deposits were $108,414. Just two years later in January, the deposits had more than doubled to $253,228. The rest of the year was not so rosy. Deposits dropped to $174,625 by December as the company experienced "The Panic of 1907," triggered by the failure of a large New York bank and runs on several of its affiliate banks. As news about the rushes spread, customers of other banks raced to withdraw funds from their own financial institutions, including a minor run on the Bank of Lumberton. McLean began to think that some action by the federal government to better control currency could stop future panics.

When the "Panic of 1907" subsided, deposits started going up again, and McLean thanked his farmer depositors in a number of ways. In 1909, the Bank of Lumberton awarded cash prizes of fifty dollars, thirty dollars and twenty dollars for the top three farmers raising the largest number of bushels of corn on one acre in Robeson County. The bank also recognized the power of economic development. It donated fifty dollars to the purchase of a mill site to bring the Kingsdale Lumber Company to Lumberton.

By 1910, the bank's deposits had reached $304,000 with total assets listed $510,223. McLean had accumulated 138 shares of stock, making him the largest single stockholder. The next largest stockholder was cashier C. B. Townsend with one hundred shares.

GROWTH COMES QUICKLY

The Bank of Lumberton was growing quickly, and it soon became evident that the small building it had occupied just a few years earlier was no longer adequate. The board voted in 1913 to build a larger, more impressive building one block away on the corner of Elm Street and Third Avenue. A bid of $20,500 was accepted for the construction of the Bank of Lumberton's second building.

During this same period, McLean's political and public service career was becoming more active. The Democrat served in various local and state political posts that brought him in contact with national politicians. Several years earlier, at 22, he was Robeson County Democratic Party chairman. He served as a delegate to the Democratic national nominating convention three times, a position that introduced him to Woodrow Wilson. When Wilson became president in 1912, he brought McLean to Washington to serve as Undersecretary of the Treasury with Treasury Secretary William Gibbs McAdoo.

FEDERAL RESERVE ACT

It was in Washington that McLean started work on legislation that would have a major impact on banking, not only in Lumberton and North Carolina, but also across the nation. Ever since the country had been founded, various presidents had pushed for a national banking system that would bring some order to the country's finances. After the "Panic of 1907" resulted in widespread bank and business failures, Congress established a National Monetary Commission. After years of debate, the commission proposed a type of central bank for the United States.

McAdoo and his assistant McLean wholeheartedly supported the central banking system, to be called the Federal Reserve System. Besides creating a sense of financial security guaranteed by the federal government, the Federal Reserve would provide facilities for discounting commercial credits and would act as a federal government supervisor of all the nationally chartered banks that chose to join. Financial crises might not be eliminated, but they could be better controlled if there were some type of national standards.

Within months after the Federal Reserve Act was passed in 1913, McLean, who had retained the bank presidency though he was living in Washington full-time, proposed that the Bank of Lumberton become the National Bank of Lumberton. The stockholders unanimously approved the change in September 1914, making it one of the first banks in the country to join the Federal Reserve System.

THE DEATH OF ANGUS MCLEAN

In April 1935, McLean was hospitalized with a blood clot in his lung. On May 17, he was on a trip to Atlantic City, New Jersey, when he was stricken again. He was rushed back to Washington by airplane.

On June 21, 1935, Angus Wilton McLean, business builder, died quietly sitting in a wheelchair. The governor, bank president, railroad founder, cotton mill builder and North Carolina Democratic Party chairman was sixty-five years old. He was survived by his wife, Margaret, and three children, Angus II, twenty-two; Margaret, nineteen; and Hector, fourteen. The news made the front pages of all of the newspapers in North Carolina, as well as the *New York Times* and *Washington Post*. ■

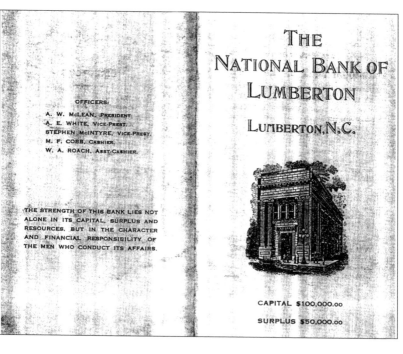

OFFICERS:

A. W. McLEAN, President
A. E. WHITE, Vice-Prest.
STEPHEN McINTYRE, Vice-Prest.
M. F. COBB, Cashier.
W. A. ROACH, Asst-Cashier.

THE STRENGTH OF THIS BANK LIES NOT ALONE IN ITS CAPITAL, SURPLUS AND RESOURCES, BUT IN THE CHARACTER AND FINANCIAL RESPONSIBILITY OF THE MEN WHO CONDUCT ITS AFFAIRS.

THE
NATIONAL BANK OF
LUMBERTON
LUMBERTON, N.C.

CAPITAL $100,000.00

SURPLUS $50,000.00

This Bank of Lumberton brochure from 1924 boasted capital of one hundred thousand dollars and a surplus of fifty thousand dollars.

CHAPTER VI

Branch Banking Company

In 1900, only three years after the Bank of Lumberton had opened for business, Branch Banking Company started operating for the first time under a charter. The statement of condition for the year 1900 showed $352,723 in assets and a capital base of $73,683. All of the stock was held by the widow and children of Alpheus Branch. Following is a list of shares held of January 10, 1900.

Shareholder	Shares
Mrs. Nannie B. Branch	38
Mrs. Mattie B. Williams	36
Alpheus Paul Branch	36
R.B. Briggs, Trustee, Ximena Briggs	36
Mrs. Nannie B. Branch, Guardian, Nannie Branch	118
Mrs. Nannie B. Branch, Guardian, Ellen M. Branch	118
Mrs. Nannie B. Branch, Guardian, Joshua Branch	118
	500

THE TURN OF THE CENTURY BRINGS PROSPERITY

In spite of dire predictions, the tobacco market had brought prosperity to Wilson, and by 1901, "... the increasing flow of buggies and carts was beginning to make Wilson one of the busiest towns in the state. Business continued as usual during Sunday as it did during any other day of the week."[1]

The gold and silver controversies that had raged through every political contest in the latter part of the nineteenth century had finally been resolved, and the nation was on a gold standard. The turn of the century brought prosperity and a more stable economic system than the country had ever known. President Theodore Roosevelt said, "The Treasury of the public is in excellent condition. Never before has the per capita of circulation been as large as it is this day, and this circulation, moreover, is of money every dollar

The vault in the neo-classical building in Wilson, N.C., that was built as
The Branch Banking Company's headquarters in 1903. It was the first structure
in Wilson County placed on the National Register of Places. In 2012, the vault was still
in the building and is used by the Wilson Arts Council.

of which is at par with gold. Now, our having this sound currency system is of benefit to banks, of course, but it is of infinitely more benefit to the people as a whole, because of the healthy effect on business conditions."[2]

The Branch Banking Company opened a savings department on December 20, 1902, and had expanded enough by the following year to require new quarters. In 1903 the bank purchased the property at the corner of Nash and Goldsboro streets[3] and built the building that served as the home office for many years.

HENRY GROVES CONNOR

Henry Groves Connor was president of the Branch Banking Company from 1900 until 1907, when he resigned to devote his full time to his duties as an associate justice of the Supreme Court of North Carolina. Numerous records indicate that Judge Connor was a well-loved man throughout his life and distinguished himself as a public servant. He is described by a contemporary as a man of "magnetic personality … lofty character and great legal ability … He had the moral courage to stand by his guns and go down in defeat if necessary rather than surrender one iota of a principle in which he believed. And his very name was a tower of strength to the forces of moral righteousness in our State." [4]

Judge Connor was a staunch Democrat all his life, but he was so well thought of by all parties that in 1909 he was appointed by Republican President Taft to the bench of the United States District Court for the Eastern District. Years later, ex-President Taft spoke at the Women's Club of Wilson and in his opening remarks said that he was glad to be in the home town of Judge Connor "… where he found that at least one of his official acts had given universal satisfaction."[5]

From 1900 until 1907 the country enjoyed general prosperity. One writer commented that after 1900, "Agriculture and industry seemed to take on new life."[6] In 1900 there were 129 banking units in North Carolina with aggregate resources of $27,000,000, and this rose sharply in seven years to 315 units with resources of $82,000,000.[7] Private banks, which had been of first importance following the War Between the States, dwindled in importance during the first decade of the twentieth century. In North Carolina twenty-eight were in operation in 1900, and only two in 1910.[8]

Advertisement in the *Wilson Times*, December 25, 1903.

CAPITAL, $100,000.00   Surplus and Profits $30,000:

BRANCH BANKING COMPANY
of Wilson,

IN OUR NEW QUARTERS

We are better than ever prepared to take care of Deposits, and hope to count every reader of this advertisement among our Depositors. By depositing your money in the bank

You Save Yourself and Family the Anxiety and Danger of Keeping it About Your House or Person.

We have a separate Vault with Safe Deposit Boxes for rent, where you can keep any Valuable Papers or Jewery, Deeds, Mortgages, Insurance Policies safe from fire. We invite you to call and examine these Boxes.

In Our Savings Department
We receive Deposits in any amount from 25c up and
PAY FOUR PER CENT. INTEREST COMPOUNDED   EVERY   THREE
MONTHS.

On April 1st, July 1st, October 1st, and on January the 1st.

In every year on all amounts that have remained on Deposit the previou three months or over. Every man, woman an child should keep a Saving Account and keep adding to it every week, no matter how little. It will grow big after awhile.

Every courtesy and cosideration shown all callers. We will be glad to talk with any one interested in any of our Departments.

BRANCH BANKING COMPANY

...in 1904

THE TRUST DEPARTMENT

Prior to 1900 there was virtually no trust business conducted in North Carolina by institutions. The Fidelity Savings and Trust Company of Durham (later the Fidelity Bank) received the first charter with fiduciary powers in 1887 and organized in 1888. The Wilmington Savings and Trust Company received its charter in 1888, though no trust work was handled by this bank until many years later.[9]

The Wilson Banking and Trust Company (now Branch Banking and Trust Company) was issued a charter in 1889. Though the charter did not define fiduciary powers, it granted the bank power to organize a savings and trust department. In 1903 and 1907 the laws of North Carolina were changed and those companies engaged in trust activities were placed under the jurisdiction of the North Carolina Corporation Commission.[10] It became necessary to receive permission from this commission before opening a trust department. In 1907 the bank's charter was amended and fiduciary powers were granted in accordance with the new laws. That year the bank opened a trust department, thus becoming among the first in the state to engage actively in trust activities.

The minutes of May 18, 1907, state, "Whereas at the late Legislature the Charter of this Bank was amended in accordance with instructions of the last Annual Meeting of the stockholders under which amendment this Bank is authorized to act as Executor, Administrator and/or in any fiduciary capacity and where such amendment provides that some officer be designated to qualify in such cases. Therefore be it resolved that the President and in his absence, the Vice President or Cashier be authorized to duly qualify in such matters as pertain to the Trust Department." Though the bank did handle trust business, it was not until 1913 that a full-time trust officer was employed. That year the bank's name was changed to incorporate this activity.

MR. HALES HANDLES A CRISIS

Jacob Cecil Hales became president during one of the most critical years that the bank ever experienced, but he was to prove himself well qualified to handle the crisis. Late in 1907 the economic situation in the United States became grave and culminated in a panic. It was called the "money panic" because there was an actual scarcity of money, thus causing many banks to use scrip in place of cash. The nation's money supply was based on Federal bonds deposited with the Secretary of the Treasury, who issued National Bank Notes. Though sound in theory, this system lacked the elasticity demanded by seasonal requirements. The panic of 1907 unveiled this weakness, as well as the danger of having money reserves concentrated in a few large cities.[11]

The *Raleigh News and Observer* gave the following account:

> *On November 2, 1907, the bankers and merchants of Greensboro, at a joint meeting, decided to issue clearing house certificates in denominations of from one to twenty dollars which were guaranteed by all of the eight banks of the city. It was further decided that not over ten dollars would be paid in cash on any one check. On November 4, the bankers of Wilson agreed to a similar plan. In Wilson the banks were prohibited from paying over twenty-five dollars in cash in any one day or one hundred dollars in any one week on checking accounts, and ten dollars in any one day or twenty-five dollars in any one week on savings accounts to the same depositor.[12]*

The minutes of November 1907 mentioned "general financial stringency"[13] and in December President Hales felt called upon to offer reassurance to the bank's New York correspondent, Hanover National Bank. He wrote to the cashier, "In times like this when there is more or less distrust and scrutiny, we have thought it prudent to have special examination of our papers by the Board of Directors and we enclose you herewith a statement over their signature for your files."

Later that month he reported to the stockholders that the Bank had "safely passed through the worst financial panic ever experienced."[14] At this same meeting a committee was appointed to study the possibility of becoming a national bank. Two years later, the motion was made and carried to become a national bank,[15] and the name "The State National Bank of Wilson" was selected.[16] However, in 1910 it was decided to defer the conversion,[17] and no further mention of it was made in the minutes. Obviously the decision then, as now, was to remain a state bank.

EDUCATIONAL CONTEST
Branch Banking Company
WILSON, N. C.

We offer prizes to two children not over 15 years old, in each township in Wilson county, who write the best Composition on George Washington. We have tried to reach every school teacher in the county to get the number of children 15 years old and under, so we could give each child a picture of George Washington, with conditions of this contest. Several teachers have not sent in the number of children, and as we want every one to have a trial we want each child who does not get a picture to have their teacher write us. Contest closes December 1.

BRANCH BANKING CO.

Advertisement in the *Wilson Times*, November 20, 1908.

...SEVERAL REASONS...
WHY YOU SHOULD KEEP A BANK ACCOUNT.

1st —

Payments by check will save you time and money in making settlements and avoids trouble and disputes about them afterwards. A Bank Account also saves you and your family risk, anxiety and danger of keeping money about your homes and person and furnishes you a record of all your financial transactions.

WHY YOU SHOULD USE THIS BANK.

2nd —

Money deposited with us can always be checked out or called for an any time. We are liberal and accommodating without carelessness; and prudent and conservative without narrowness. We safe guard every dollar deposited with us and take no risk whatever necessary or unnecessary. We are amply able and willing to serve you in any banking business.

At the beginning of another new crop season we offer our services and facilities to our farming friends throughout Wilson and adjoining counties and if you are not already a depositor with us we hope to add your name to the 3,000 already on our books.

BRANCH BANKING COMPANY
J. C. HALES, President.   H. H. MURRAY, Cashier.
WILSON, N. C.

BRANCH BANKING COMPANY, OF WILSON, N. C.

Advertisement in the *Wilson Times*, August 16, 1912.

President Hales had been associated with the bank since 1889, and in 1910 the stockholders issued engraved invitations to a ceremony held at the bank to present to him "a testimonial of their appreciation of his services to the Bank and to the people of the community during the past twenty-one years."

Mr. Hales was a scholarly man, deeply religious, and was acclaimed as one of Wilson's best-loved citizens. His own words give a clear insight into his character:

> *Competition in the Banking business is fierce and manysided. We experience some that is not altogether fair and professional tho' I assure you we never resort to any such methods. We attend strictly to our own business and I believe one reason for the success of our effort is that we never overlook an old customer's interest in our efforts to gain new business. We never throw over our old friends for new ones. We want new ones all the time but not at the expense of old ones. Courtesy, consideration, kindness and accommodation rightly distributed pays good interest in the long run. Sometimes a customer of small consequence in himself will be the means of bringing in good business in his contact with others. Every one counts some.[18]*

ANXIOUS DAYS REMEMBERED

The year 1911 was an "off-year." The price of tobacco dropped and this affected adversely all other businesses, though the situation changed in 1912. Assets that year were reported at $1,248,303, almost double what they had been in 1907 when Mr. Hales became president, and three-and-a-half times greater than they had been in 1900.

> *With unusual seasons both for the working and harvesting of abundant crops, with good prices for cotton, and the highest prices ever known for tobacco, Nineteen Hundred and Twelve will long be recalled by the people of Wilson County as a year when every farmer, tenant as well as landlord, prospered as they never prospered before.*
>
> *There is today in the banks and in the pockets and homes of people more than twice the money than was ever before in the county. The money assets in this county had doubled in the last*

four short months. This has been a wonderful opportunity for the Bank, and, realizing it very early in the fall, we grasped the opportunity, and have taken advantage of it to the fullest extent, as shown by our recent statement. We have more money on deposit than all the banks in Wilson put together, and nearly as much as all the banks in Wilson County put together.

The increased deposits and the accumulation of large sums of money, while it brings a larger sphere of usefulness and a greater degree of responsibility, it also eliminates one great source of anxiety and worry and responsibility in the way of rediscounting heavily North.[19]

Mr. Hales became reminiscent in this report and revealed the perils that the bank had escaped in former years:

Only a few years ago, our rediscounts every summer would exceed our deposits. This state of things was always a source of great anxiety, but the business required it. Out of it we have emerged into a state of comparative plenty. I recall many and many a summer when we would anxiously count the months before we could expect any money from the crops, and wonder if we would get through. Along in July when we would feel that we had called on our correspondent banks for about all we could expect, we would even count the days; and every day passed would be that much off our minds. We would feel like one working on a precipice, when any accident would render our life work a failure. Day after day this anxiety would be with us, go with us to our meals, lie down with us at night and wake up with us in the morning; and through it all we would have to keep a smiling face and never let the inquiring customer feel that it was any trouble to accommodate him. It is a spirit of thankfulness that I feel that those trying summers are gone, and gone I hope never to come again. Nevermore, I hope, will Wilson County have to leave her borders to secure money to work her farms, finance her factories or accommodate her merchants.[20] ∎

CHAPTER VII

Branch Banking and Trust Company
1913-1933

A NEW NAME AND A NEW PRESIDENT

As the younger Bank of Lumberton prepared to move into a larger building in 1913, Branch Banking Company was preparing for change as well. That same year, the Wilson bank renamed its company Branch Banking and Trust Company and elected Shelby Hurt Anderson as president following the death of its top executive, J. C. Hales.

Mr. Anderson, born on February 4, 1874, in Halifax County, Virginia, and came to Wilson as a young man in his early twenties. He and his brother, Will P., founded Watson Warehouse when the tobacco industry was still young in Wilson.

MONETARY REFORMS

The national banking system in 1913 was 50 years old. It had been designed in 1863 as a wartime expedient to meet the demands of a country at war with itself. It was not successful, nor did it meet the demands of normal trade in later years.[1] On three occasions (1873, 1893 and 1907), its inadequacies brought on financial disasters throughout the land, thereby causing the system to be termed the "panic breeder."[2]

It was sound, but it did not change in volume with the requirements of business. Just at the time when a local bank in a rural area needed a larger volume of currency to aid in moving crops into markets or in an industrial area to meet the needs of manufacturers and merchants for expansion, it could not secure United States bonds on which to expand its supply of bank notes ...[3]

Advertisements that ran in the *Wilson Times* in 1915.

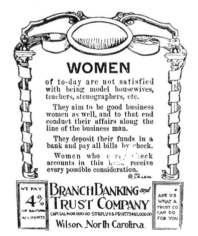

After the financial chaos of 1907, Congress created the National Monetary Commission to carry on a thorough investigation of monetary systems. It took four years for this commission to complete its investigation and to turn in a report.[4] Finally, in December 1913, the Federal Reserve Act was passed, the nation's fourth attempt to provide a satisfactory monetary system. The Federal Reserve System was to issue to member banks Federal Reserve Notes that were secured by discounted paper, a vast improvement over the former system. These Federal Reserve Notes eventually replaced the National Bank Notes. The new system eliminated some significant problems; however, it also created risk of its own and contributed to the Great Depression.

SIDNEY GRAHAM MEWBORN

The year 1915 brought both large and small changes to the bank. S. H. Anderson was elevated to chairman of the board, and Sidney Graham Mewborn became president.[5]

Mr. Mewborn, a native of Greene County, began his practice of law in Wilson after his graduation from the University of North Carolina. Immediately prior to being elected president, he served the county as clerk of the Superior Court.

That year the bank bought its first posting and statement machine[6] and advertised that it was now providing an additional service for its customers— monthly statements. The bank's new policy of keeping the savings department open until 9 on Saturday nights[7] seems harsh by today's standards, but it is somewhat softened by a later "motion made and carried to close bank Saturday Oct-30-1915 at 12:30 account Barnum and Bailey's circus."[8] Indeed, the arrival of the circus was an event of some importance in 1915!

WORLD WAR I

America's entry into World War I was noted in the minutes of 1917:

The past year has been in many respects an unusual and an eventful one; though, in a large degree national rather than state or local or sectional. Since our last meeting our country has actually joined the cause of the Allies and has been for some eight

*months actively engaged in this world war. As usual, finances
have been disturbed from normal to abnormal or war conditions.
Money has been more plentiful and possessing less purchasing
power than certainly since the Civil War.*

*One of the great events of the year has been the two successful
Liberty Bond sales by the United States Government ... The
selling, handling and distribution of these bonds has imposed an
enormous burden and task upon our banks, which have acted as
the direct agencies for the selling and distribution of these bonds.
Our own Bank has faithfully and fully discharged its part of this
immense task. For ourselves and subscribers we have purchased
$275,000.00 of these bonds.*[9]

As is usual, the war created many demands for products and food. In April
the *Daily Times* began putting in large headlines above its masthead:
"PLANT EVERY AVAILABLE FOOT OF LAND IN FOOD CROPS."

President Mewborn said of the year 1917, "One of the satisfactory results
of the year's workings of the bank has been its widening influence and high
reputation as a 'BIG BANK,' one of the big institutions of the State, this Bank
is regarded as ranking among the highest and strongest financial institutions
in this section."[10]

As the demands for products and food were met, prices soared. All types of
producers found markets for their products and in 1919, the war over,
prosperity seemed to have arrived.[11] The Wilson tobacco market climbed to
an all-time high of $53.67* per hundred pounds, which it was not to reach
again until 1950. The bank's assets jumped to $4,878,540 from $2,597,345
the preceding year.

Though there was a recession in 1920-21, banks in North Carolina expanded
greatly during the period from 1914 to 1923. In 1914 aggregate resources
of North Carolina banks were $153,114,438[12] and in 1923 they were
$491,325,000,[13] an increase of 221%. During this same period, Branch
Banking and Trust Company expanded from $1,067,357 to $4,346,527—
an increase of 307%.

---

* The average for the preceding five years was $22.53.

PROGRESS IN THE 1920s

The 1920s saw Branch Banking and Trust Company make great strides forward in every area of activity. Resources increased 64%, and deposits jumped 119%. Four permanent new offices were established and an insurance department was opened in November, 1922, with D. W. Kellogg as manager, a position he held until his retirement on December 31, 1961.

Early in the decade, the *Daily Times* described Wilson's banks as:

> ... *strong, well buttressed against the stress of the time, conservatively managed against the dangers of over confidence in times of prosperity, yet managed with a spirit of service to the community and to their depositors ... This fact is clearly demonstrated by the success, the substantial growth, and the volume of business transacted through the Branch Banking and Trust Company. This sterling financial institution ranks high not only among Southern banks, but of those of the entire nation.*[14]

HERBERT DALTON BATEMAN

S. G. Mewborn resigned as president in 1924 to accept an appointment as judge of the Wilson County General Court. He was succeeded by Herbert Dalton Bateman, who had been with the bank since 1916 as cashier and vice president. Mr. Bateman saw the bank through the trying period ahead and, as president, he helped to establish policies that enabled the bank to weather the nation's worst economic storm.

BANKS OF WILSON

During the 1920s and early 30s, eight banks operated in the City of Wilson. Branch Banking and Trust Company was the only one that survived the financial disasters of the early 1930s.

TABLE IV[15]
Banks Established in Wilson Prior to 1931

Bank	Opened	Closed
Branch Banking and Trust Company	1872	—
First National Bank of Wilson (Reopened July 15, 1932 as National Bank of Wilson)	Feb. 16, 1874	Dec. 29, 1931
Wilson Trust and Savings Bank	July 2, 1903	Dec. 29, 1931
Citizens Bank	Jan. 2. 1906	1927 merged with Planters Bank
Planters Bank	Mar. 10, 1917	Dec. 28, 1931
Farmers Banking and Trust Company	Sept. 7, 1920	Mar. 3, 1927 merged with Planters Bank
Commercial Bank	Mar. 31, 1921	Sept. 23, 1929
North Carolina Industrial Bank	Aug. 30, 1930	Mar. 31, 1934

THE OPENING OF BRANCH OFFICES, 1921-1931

Branch Banking and Trust Company was one of the first large institutions in this section of the country to venture extensively into "branch banking," though the term is purely coincidental. Prior to the War Between the States, branch banking was popular among state chartered banks in North Carolina, but only four banks operated branches between the years 1865 and 1900.[16] From 1900 to 1928 the total grew to 26, and of these, Branch Banking and Trust Company operated four.

The establishment of branch offices by Branch Banking and Trust Company began in 1921 with an office at Bailey,17 which was later discontinued. Plymouth, the oldest existing office, was opened January 29, 1925, and was followed by Warsaw on May 24, 1926, and Selma on January 1, 1928. During this period an office was opened at Whitakers, but like Bailey, it was later discontinued.

On January 25, 1929, an office was opened at Goldsboro. The stock market crash at the end of that year did not halt the bank's expansion program. On January 17, 1930, the Fayetteville office opened, and on February 13 the bank bought Farmers and Merchants Bank at Williamston. The New Bern office opened on August 9, 1930. On May 7, 1931, an office was opened at Kinston and on May 16 it was decided to consolidate the Toisnot Banking Company at Elm City with the bank.

ISOLATIONISM

In the era following World War I the nations of the world tried to maintain internal prosperity by economic isolation. High tariff barriers became even higher, and Russia went to the extreme of forbidding any foreign trade. Each nation seemed to think it could stand alone, or at least live within its own borders. The American government encouraged foreign loans and exports but discouraged imports and succeeded for a while in casting the United States in the role of creditor nation for the world.[18]

The government also encouraged vast internal improvement, such as new highways and huge public buildings, which, of course, were paid for by loans. Different types of credit came into their own – installment buying, purchase of stock on margin, and real estate bonds.[19]

A tide of "get rich quickism" swept over the nation in the 1920s. It was not uncommon for a person to withdraw his life savings to buy stocks, or to buy on margin where possible. The new daily heights that the stocks reached only served to spur others on to greater recklessness in stock purchases. Everyone discussed stocks and the fantastic fortunes made, or reputed to have been made.

BRANCH INVESTMENT COMPANY

The prosperity that farmers enjoyed during the war and post war period encouraged banks throughout the nation to invest heavily in farm mortgages. On July 6, 1921, Branch Bank and Metropolitan Life Insurance Company signed a contract whereby Metropolitan agreed to discount Branch Bank's first mortgages.[20] In 1923 a department was established for this function and was called the Investment Department, later known as the Mortgage Loan Department.[21]

As the 1920s wore on, it became more and more difficult to convert mortgages into cash, even on those properties that were considered good investments. Branch Banking and Trust Company was forced to take second mortgages, and on April 15, 1929, established Branch Investment Company to purchase both first and second mortgages from the bank, thereby protecting the bank's investments as well as those of the Metropolitan Life Insurance Company. The company continued in existence until September 28, 1933,[22] when the crisis was safely over.

ECONOMIC TRAGEDY

Toward the end of the decade, the many factors that were laying a treacherous groundwork for the crash of 1929 were ignored or misinterpreted, even by economists. A great surplus of cotton, wheat, coal and silver existed. Many banks failed, especially in rural areas, though the metropolitan areas and other large segments of the country seemed to be prosperous.

The tobacco market in Wilson began its gradual decline in 1927, dropped to $13.82 in 1930 compared with an average of $24.62 for the decade. It dipped to $9.03 in 1931, the lowest it had been since 1909.

O. Max Gardner, Governor of North Carolina, wrote:

> *The good times stopped. The panic did not wait until 1931 to strike North Carolina. The fog and darkness, forerunning our present economic upset, were gradually settling over the state even before the crash of 1929. One of the most serious aspects of the intricate maze of interlocking difficulties that the state was grappling with, and that we lumped together under the head of economic depression, was the fact that North Carolina agriculture had become unprofitable.*[23]

The gradual decline in the stock market began two months before October 1929, but did not seem alarming to the general public. Though the crash caused speculation to come to a sudden end, no one anticipated the depths that the resulting depression was to reach. The day after the crash, the *Daily Times* published an article stating that in the opinion of the state bank examiners the financial health of North Carolina was good and that the banks had not been affected by the crash to any marked degree. Most North Carolina banks had resisted the temptation to invest at high rates of interest in New York, preferring to lend the money at home for the usual six percent.[24]

In the same edition, Editor John D. Gold said, "The stock market has gone to pieces and perhaps legitimate business will now have a chance."[25] At the stockholders meeting in January of 1930, President Bateman reported that the bank had a good year despite the depressed conditions existing in the country.

A RUN ON WILSON BANKS

From January 1930 to January 1932, 131 state banks in North Carolina failed. A run developed on the Wilson banks on December 28, 1931, and the following day Planters Bank did not open for business. This closure caused intensified withdrawals on the three remaining banks. On December 29, the First National Bank of Wilson and the Wilson Trust and Savings Bank decided not to open the following day, causing drastic withdrawals from Branch Banking and Trust Company on December 30.

The mob scene of that day is well remembered by everyone who witnessed it. Traffic was stopped, and people filled the streets and lined up at every door of Branch Banking and Trust Company, Wilson's only remaining bank. Witnesses say that the crowd was orderly, though there was some pushing and shoving. Mostly people were just concerned—concerned about their life's savings. They swapped places in line, sometimes bargaining for preferred positions.

The bank paid in full the demands of each depositor as he reached the head of the line. Many customers withdrew funds, took them immediately to the Post Office and deposited them in Postal Savings. Customers were unaware that the Post Office officials went out the back door with this same money and deposited it at Branch Banking and Trust Company. So, during these crucial hours the same cash was paid out over and over.

The situation called for delay, though not apparent delay. Assistant Cashier W. G. Smith is said to have examined each bill carefully, and he counted and recounted cash before releasing it to a customer. All of the officers knew that cash had been ordered and was on the way, but none knew when it would arrive. One bank official remembers cash in the vault getting lower and lower as the morning wore on and finally, he could stand it no longer. He burst into tears.

Only moments later, a Brinks' truck came to a screeching halt at the front door, and the crowd saw bags of money being carried into the bank by armed guards. A bank employee lettered a large sign and posted it in front of the bank. It read, "We have $1,000,000. Come and get it!"

Some people in the crowd became reassured and before long there was a line for deposits as well as one for withdrawals.

The tide had turned. Editor John D. Gold urged those who were hoarding money to put it back in the bank for their own safety. Naturally, robberies did occur in the days that followed.

The fact that two million dollars were drawn out of three banks of Wilson causing them to close is sufficient evidence that there is money around, no matter where it is, whether in the cupboard, corner, or buried in the earth.[26]

In January 1932 a resolution was passed by the directors in Goldsboro that expressed the sentiments of those involved in the unhappy days of the preceding year:

Resolved, that we commend the efficient management of the Branch Banking and Trust Company during the year 1931, and in particular do we commend the president, H. D. Bateman, for his far sighted banking vision in keeping the bank in such sound and safe condition, and the fine way he had handled the situation during the recent crisis.[27]

By 1932 the depression, which got its impetus from the stock market crash, could no longer be termed a temporary setback. Between June 1931 and June 1932, 2,427 of the nation's banks had failed.[28] The Senate appointed a committee to investigate banking and finance, and their unfavorable findings were publicized widely in newspapers and on the radio. It would seem that unsound banking practices were not uncommon.

In retrospect, it is clear that the Federal Reserve System itself was a major cause of the long duration of the Great Depression. The Federal Reserve reduced the money supply drastically in the 1920s, which contributed to bank failures, after over expanding money in the early and mid-1920s. Also, by having one national system, the Federal Reserve spread the panic to the whole country. In the past, economic corrections had been severe but short-lived, as the free market quickly responded to the new conditions. As a federal bureaucracy, the Federal Reserve responded slowly and often destructively.

By March 2, 1933, 22 states saw fit to suspend or to limit banking operations.* Roosevelt's inauguration was on March 4, and one of his first acts was to declare a bank holiday to be effective March 5 through March 9.

Application had to be made to authorities before any bank was allowed to reopen after the bank holiday. Branch Banking and Trust Company did so immediately and reopened on March 15, 1933.[29]

On March 10 the *Daily Times* printed an editorial which, in effect, gave a tongue lashing to the citizens of Wilson:

> *The country is now getting a lesson in credits, values and banking that it has not had in many years ... The folks are beginning to understand that the financial and credit structure of the country is very intricate and vast in proportions, and when the system is out of gear it takes some time to get it properly adjusted.*

> *For two years or more people have been hoarding money and the withdrawal of this money from the channels of business has had a disastrous effect upon the financial affairs of the nation and world.*

> *Those who draw their money from banks and then expect to borrow from them, when they are in need, find that the other fellow is doing the same thing and this restricts the ability of the bank to lend.*

> *During these days while the banks are closed much of the money that is being spent is coming out of safety deposit boxes and places of hiding, and the merchants say that business is good considering conditions. That means that all over this country the people who are unable to get money out of banks are taking it out of their hiding places.[30]*

> *Since our banks here are as sound as can be, and with ample money to meet all the demands of their depositors, let's bring business back in Wilson by placing our money in our banks and show to all the world that Wilson looks confidently to the future, and expects from now on to build in every way.[31]*

It is interesting to note that during the most crucial period of banking history the resources of Branch Banking and Trust Company rose steadily and the bank continued to open branch offices, while the aggregate resources of North Carolina banks declined, as did the number of banking units. ■

* North Carolina's State Commissioner of Banks, Gurney Hood, refused to do so.

TABLE V[32]
Comparison of Resources and Banking Units
of North Carolina Banks and
Branch Banking and Trust Company, 1929-1933

Year	*North Carolina Banks**		*Branch Bank*	
	Resources	Units	Resources	Units
1929	$ 465,269,000	489	$ 4,724,678	5
1930	361,139,000	400	5,426,635	8
1931	296,997,000	365	6,386,168	10
1932	263,224,000	336	7,694,762	10
1933	257,280,000	287	13,772,634	11

* State and National.

CHAPTER VIII

Branch Banking and Trust Company
1933-1952

THE GOVERNMENT STEPS IN

The government under Roosevelt's administration was galvanized into action, and he sped much legislation through Congress regulating almost every phase of banking. The temporary Federal Deposit Insurance Fund was set up under the Banking Act of 1933 and in 1935 became the permanent Federal Deposit Insurance Corporation, which insured deposits up to $5,000 (now $250,000).[1] All banks in the country were required to join before they could reopen after the bank holiday.

RECONSTRUCTION FINANCE CORPORATION

Late in 1933 Branch Banking and Trust Company amended its charter to provide for preferred stock with a total par value of $400,000, which was subsequently sold to the Reconstruction Finance Corporation.[2] This corporation, established in 1932, was a government loan agency designed to lend aid to basic industries, such as banking, insurance firms and railroads.[3] In 1933 it was authorized to purchase preferred stock, a hitherto unused type of stock in banking organizations,[4] though sale of this stock was not restricted to the Reconstruction Finance Corporation.

In 1949 the capital structure of Branch Banking and Trust Company showed only common stock, the preferred stock having been redeemed.

THE RECOVERY BEGINS

It has been said that North Carolina enjoyed a more rapid recovery than did other sections of the United States. This has been attributed to the fact that in both agriculture and manufacturing, the products, cotton and cotton goods, tobacco and tobacco products, were primarily consumer goods with a relatively inelastic demand which required relatively small expenditures on the part of the individual.[5] From 1900 to 1937, North Carolina's wealth increased 580%, greater than any other state.[6]

After the bank holiday, bank deposits started their climb back up as the public regained its confidence in the American banking system. Banks, following the dictates of a still shaky economy, were cautious in the types and amounts of loans made, and the average person was reluctant to obligate himself by borrowing from a bank because of an uncertain economic future. Therefore, some banks had surplus funds on hand.

This, coupled with the government's restriction on bank purchases of corporate bonds, resulted in a gradual increase in investments in municipal bonds, which were more plentiful because of the liquidated assets of those banks that failed to reopen.

THE BOND DEPARTMENT

On October 7, 1931, BB&T obtained a license from the State of North Carolina to operate as a security dealer. S. S. Lawrence, who had been cashier since 1927, was chosen to formulate and head the new Bond Department. Its functions then were to invest the bank's surplus funds and to buy and sell bonds—particularly municipal bonds—for the bank and its customers.

Mr. Lawrence was regarded as one of the foremost bond market specialists in the nation and his expertise was instrumental in keeping the bank on a solid foundation during trying times. Reluctance on the part of individuals and businesses to borrow money and the reluctance on the part of bank officials to accept any appreciable risk led to the bank's reliance on the Bond Department to produce the major part of income and profits.

THE TRUST DEPARTMENT

E. B. Crow, who was a certified public accountant, joined the staff in 1930 as an auditor. Five years later, he was named head of the Trust Department, a position he held for 34 years. Under his leadership, the Trust Department became one of the major divisions of the bank.

NEW BRANCH OFFICES

The operation of branch offices was becoming more and more popular throughout the state, and by the end of 1935 forty-five were in existence,[7] eleven of which were owned and operated by Branch Banking and Trust Company.

On August 30, 1933, the Wallace office was opened, and on December 20, 1934, an office was established at Trenton. That same year Branch Banking and Trust Company remodeled the home office in Wilson and purchased property behind this building, where upon it constructed another building connected with the original structure.

The office at Faison was opened on May 7, 1936, and on January 29, 1938, the bank took over the operation of the Bank of Fremont, which had previously closed.

After this time, however, World War II intervened, and it was not until 1949 that another branch was established.

WORLD WAR II

During the 1940s and 1950s several abnormal factors influenced the amount of money deposited in banks throughout the country. As was natural, World War II caused resources to increase greatly. For example, the resources of Branch Banking and Trust Company at the end of 1941 were $32,728,599 and during the following year increased by $27,831,833, making a total of $60,560,432. Since the government spent billions on the war effort, more money was in circulation and employment reached an all-time high. In addition, the normal expenditures that a family would have for such things as new automobiles were not made because no automobiles were manufactured during the war years. Therefore, money was kept in banks until such time as these products became available.

In speaking of the increase in resources during 1942, President Bateman said to the stockholders: "You, no doubt, will wonder where all of this increase came from, and in this connection, I might say that it came from all over Eastern North Carolina. We have our full share, to be sure, of the local business. The greatest problem in connection with our large line of deposits

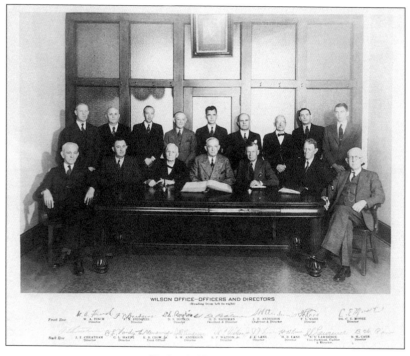

The Board of Directors, 1938

is the profitable investment of same. There are practically no demands for good bankable loans. This situation forces us to take very low yields from Government bonds …"[8]

Another factor that influenced the abnormal growth of deposits during the war was the purchase of government bonds. When the bank purchased these bonds, the money was deposited to the credit of the federal government, thus swelling the deposit figure. Also, the deposits Branch Banking and Trust Company had from other banks rose greatly. During the war interest rates were low because money was plentiful, so there was very little inducement to invest funds in securities. As interest rates increased, other banks invested their funds rather than leaving them on deposit with correspondent banks.

POST WAR PERIOD

During the period immediately following the war, United States production of consumer products was resumed, and the public demanded from banks a resumption of installment loans, as well as regular loans. At the end of 1945, the total loans on the book of Branch Banking and Trust Company amounted to $2,733,197, and rose to $10,094,370 in 1951, which was also the year of the high watermark in securities investments. The 9 to 1 ratio of that year steadily decreased as more money went into loans with a corresponding reduction in securities.

The bond issue, which Governor W. Kerr Scott was successful in floating in the late 1940s, was an important economic factor at the time. Many miles of roads were paved, particularly secondary ones. Again, more money was in circulation, and travel for the rural population became easier, resulting in an increased number of farmers who became steady customers of banks throughout the state.

The federal government continued to spend large sums of money on internal improvements. At the end of 1949, Mr. Bateman pointed out that one United States president had spent for the preceding five years, more money than all of the 32 presidents before him. (The extraordinary expenditures of the war years 1941-1945, were excluded.)

In 1950 the Wilson tobacco market reached a high of $57.10 per hundred pounds. The average for the preceding ten-year period had been $40.53.

Both 1950 and 1951 were good tobacco years, and the number of pounds, as well as the price, increased over previous years.

Mr. Bateman reported: "The year 1950, which has just passed, was an eventful one. On June 23, we suddenly became engaged in an undeclared war and we are still in that war and no one that I can think of is able to give any possible accurate statement as to the result of same. We only know that in this country we have the beginning, and I am afraid only the beginning, of an enormous inflation, which means an increase in prices of most materials and an enormous increase in the cost of living."[9] The bank's resources increased from $99,507,980 in 1950 to $124,941,681 in 1951.

THE CORRESPONDENT BANK DEPARTMENT

Since the mid-1930s, Branch Banking and Trust Company's Correspondent Bank Department had become an important segment of the business. Regulation Q, which had been passed by the Federal Reserve Board in 1933, prohibited member banks from paying interest on demand deposits. The interpretation was that any bank that absorbed exchange was, in effect, paying interest on demand deposits. Because the Federal Deposit Insurance Corporation did not agree, it allowed non-member banks to continue as before. Since Branch Banking and Trust did absorb exchange, other banks saved considerable amounts of money by keeping on deposit sums substantial enough to warrant the absorption. Branch Banking and Trust was one of the major correspondent banks in the country and one of the few that specialized in the collection of non-par checks on an exchange absorption basis. The high watermark was reached in the early 1950s when 50 percent of the bank's deposits were those from other banks.

During this period of time, Branch Bank became known as the "Banker's Bank." Because of the high ratio of volatile bank deposits, major investments were in U.S. government and state, county and municipal bonds in order to provide the necessary and required liquidity.

GROWTH UNDER MR. BATEMAN

When Mr. Bateman took over the presidency in 1924, the bank's total resources were $3,466,252. On the day of his retirement 28 years later, resources were $121,499,001.

The first permanent branch office was established in Plymouth in 1925 under his direction. The policy of establishing branch offices continued until 1938 when it was suspended for several years due to the war and other economic considerations.

In 1949 an office was opened in Pikeville, followed by the Haymount Drive-In Branch, Fayetteville, in 1950, and the Five Points Branch, Wilson, in 1951. This brought the total number of offices to 17, all of which had been established during Mr. Bateman's tenure. ■

CHAPTER IX

Branch Banking and Trust Company
1953-1981

JOSHUA ERNEST PASCHALL

On December 31, 1952, Mr. Bateman retired from the presidency. In his October letter announcing his retirement to the board, he said: "Now, since I am preparing to retire, I feel and strongly feel, I should recommend to you the best man I think, viewing this matter from all angles, to take my place. I have given this subject much thought and deliberation and have come to the conclusion that our Vice President and Cashier, Mr. J. E. Paschall, is the best man I know to succeed me as President of the bank." His suggestion was adopted, and Joshua Ernest Paschall became president. Mr. Paschall's outstanding abilities were well known to his fellow officers and to his many banking friends throughout the nation.

Mr. Paschall instituted programs of expansion and modernization that continued after his retirement. The West Nash Street Office (later located at Wren Village) opened in 1957. The merger of the Wilson Industrial Bank into the Branch system in 1958 represented our commitment to enter the installment loan business aggressively. The Installment Loan Branch opened that year in Kinston and later was moved into new quarters on Queen Street.

In 1959 the second addition to the home office was constructed, an office was opened in Raleigh, and The Planters Bank (with offices in Stantonsburg and Saratoga) was acquired by merger.

An office in Magnolia and the Rowan Street Office in Fayetteville were the first of many to be opened during the 1960s. The Citizens Bank with offices in Micro and Princeton merged in 1961, followed the next year by six new offices: Queen Street Drive-In, Kinston (mentioned above); Black Creek; Neuse Boulevard Drive-In, New Bern; Ash Street Drive-In, Goldsboro; Cary;

State College, Raleigh. In 1963 three offices were opened: Southside, Raleigh (later the Wake Forest Road Drive-In): Roper; Eureka.

Construction on the multi-million dollar Raleigh building was well under way prior to Mr. Paschall's retirement at the end of 1963.

INDUSTRY IN EASTERN NORTH CAROLINA

Through the years, Eastern North Carolina had built its economy on one crop. Cotton predominated until just before the turn of the century, and then tobacco took over as the major money-maker. Since World War II, farming had undergone drastic changes, and the East began losing its rural population. For example, between 1950 and 1960 the rural population in North Carolina increased 2.2% but decreased 8% in Wilson County.[1] Farms produced more tobacco poundage per acre because of higher yielding varieties and better farming practices, and fewer laborers were required because of such things as improved farm machinery. The trend turned away from tenant farming, with the surplus labor force gradually drifting away from the area, taking its purchasing power with it.

Mr. Paschall believed that one method of stemming this flow was to encourage industry, especially food processing plants, to build in the East. He worked closely with former Governors Luther H. Hodges and Terry Sanford to this end. In 1957 he said:

Eastern North Carolina needs additional industrial plants to balance its economy. It has all the necessary resources for most manufacturers—labor, water, climate, land, transportation, access to the centers of population and raw materials, and other advantages ... A broad policy should be adopted and pursued vigorously with the blessing of the State Legislature and implemented whereby more industry will be attracted to the state and particularly to Eastern North Carolina. Only when this is done, and it will take years of untiring effort, will the economy of this area find a happy balance.[2]

The next year Mr. Paschall was able to report that the Legislature had altered the tax structure to entice industry to the state.

MR. PASCHALL'S TENURE

During his 11 years in the presidency, Mr. Paschall successfully guided the bank through a period of great change. He instituted a program of remodeling bank buildings and establishing new offices. He increased the number of branches from 17 to 35 and the number of cities and towns served from 15 to 25.

One of the greatest changes that occurred during Mr. Paschall's tenure was the shift in emphasis in the bank's philosophy of investments. In 1956 he employed John A. Campbell, Jr., who had been president of the South Carolina National Bank. His expertise in the area of credit administration greatly benefited the bank during this period when loan policies were undergoing substantial change.

On the day Mr. Paschall became president, loans amounted to $12,446,600 and they increased 328.5% to $53,332,013 at the end of 1963. During the same period, investment in securities decreased 25.3%, and correspondent bank balances continued their gradual decline.

The Bond Department had been established in 1931, making Branch Bank the oldest registered dealer bank in North Carolina. One month before his retirement at the end of 1963, Mr. Lawrence commented on the change in investment philosophy. He pointed out that loans had reached the same level as securities and continued by saying, "While interest from securities will continue to be a major factor in our earnings picture, it is not likely that profits will be realized to any substantial extent in the years ahead. We are now definitely back in the banking business, and with all hands pushing for loans, it behooves the Bond Department to be in position to provide the necessary cash."

The changes in policy, particularly those relating to deposits and loans, were communicated to the bank's various customers through the Advertising and Public Relations Department, which was established in 1960.

The Board of Directors selected Frederick Louis Carr as its chairman in January 1962. Mr. Carr was the grandson of the bank's founder and had been a member of the board since 1939 when he succeeded his father, who died that year. S. H. Anderson, who had been chairman since 1915, was elected honorary chairman, though he held that position only 36 days. At the age of 88, he died at his home on March 1, 1962.

Mr. Paschall was a dedicated leader in the world of banking. He served as a member of the State Banking Commission and spent a busy year in 1960-1961 as president of the North Carolina Bankers Association. Following his retirement on December 31, 1963, he was elected State Representative in the General Assembly from District 15, composed of Wilson and Johnston counties, which placed him in a position to continue to use his talents to help strengthen the economy of the entire state.

THE SOARING SIXTIES[3]

During the first half of the 1960s, an unprecedented period of sustained economic growth brought widespread prosperity without corrosive inflation. North Carolina experienced continued industrial growth, wider diversification, more employment and increased prosperity.

The latter half of the decade, however, was a discordant period of too rapid economic growth characterized by an inflationary cycle that robbed everyone of a healthy portion of his previous economic gains.

Many banks made a headlong dash for growth at any cost, and as a result, in many cases, growth in assets far outstripped their growth in capital. Branch Banking and Trust continued its emphasis on financial strength and stability, successfully avoiding many of the problems experienced by the so-called "go go" banks.

JOHN LAFAYETTE SATCHWELL

John Lafayette Satchwell succeeded Mr. Paschall as president. He had joined the Goldsboro staff in 1932 and had remained there six years until Branch Banking and Trust Company assumed the deposit liabilities of the Bank of Fremont. Mr. Satchwell was sent there to manage the Fremont Office and to liquidate the remaining assets for the Federal Deposit Insurance Corporation. In 1950 he was transferred to the Wilson home office as a vice president and was elected to the Board of Directors a year later. His exceptional abilities were quickly recognized as he assumed greater systemwide responsibilities, and in 1957 he was promoted to senior vice president and cashier. He assumed the presidency on January 1, 1964.

"Our position of leadership requires an aggressive program and alertness at every turn," Mr. Satchwell stated. "We live in a rapidly changing world where populations are constantly being reshuffled; basic occupations of the past are becoming obsolete and giving way to completely new skills. Old communities take on surprising aspects, hitherto unknown, by remolding their terrains and remaking their maps. Today there seems to be a new approach to every avenue of living, and this calls for a new approach to banking too. In order to set our sights for the future, we must begin by taking a look at North Carolina. As a result of high potentialities and modern scientific knowledge, selective and desirable industries are moving into our state. Each new factory or industrial plant offers us the opportunity to expand our usefulness."

MR. SATCHWELL'S MILESTONES

The nine years of Mr. Satchwell's presidency were marked by significant milestones in the bank's history and other equally noteworthy evidences of his capable leadership. His long tenure in the field of banking and his fund of knowledge spanning the world of business enabled him to guide the bank into new areas of service as well as new areas of the state.

Expansion and updating of facilities, operations, services and personnel policies were extensive during his administration. A Personnel Department was created in 1964, and the bank improved its retirement benefits, adopted a profit sharing plan, updated many fringe benefits and inaugurated an extensive recruiting and management training program to meet immediate and long-range needs.

A Marketing Department with research capabilities was established in 1967 and the Data Processing Department became operational in 1971.

BB&T entered the bank credit card field in 1969. The Atlantic States Bankcard Association was formed by 57 banks in North Carolina, South Carolina and Virginia to administer Master Charge (later renamed MasterCard) through a computer center located in Raleigh. Membership in Interbank made the card national and international in scope.

MERGERS

The Bank of Davie, with two offices in Mocksville, merged into Branch Banking and Trust Company in 1967, giving the bank its first opportunity to offer its services and resources to residents of the progressive Piedmont area.

The following year, the Bank of Halifax with offices in Enfield, Halifax, Littleton, Scotland Neck and Weldon merged into the system.

The merger of the Bank of Statesville into Branch Banking and Trust Company on December 31, 1970, added two new offices in the Piedmont area.

EXPANSION AND BUILDING PROGRAMS CONTINUE

The Raleigh Main Office moved into the Branch Banking and Trust Company building in 1965.

The seven-story home office building in Wilson was completed in 1971. During Open House activities, the late Honorable Edwin M. Gill, who was at that time treasurer of the State of North Carolina, stated:

> *Today I wish to congratulate the Branch Banking and Trust Company which is old in years and young in spirit; which is modern in its ability to adjust to a swiftly changing and complex world. Your bank has seen and surveyed with honor both hard times and good times, and I can think of no greater compliment to pay than to say that you have pursued the path of progress with integrity.*

New branch offices that opened during Mr. Satchwell's tenure were: North William Street Drive-In, Goldsboro, 1964; Raleigh, 1965; Washington Street Drive-In, Williamston, and Plymouth Plaza Drive-In, 1966; Beaufort, 1967; Vernon Park Mall Drive-In, Kinston, and Eastgate Drive-In, Goldsboro, 1969; Roanoke Rapids, King Shopping Center and Tallywood Shopping Center, Fayetteville, 1970; Home Office in Wilson; Crabtree Valley and Colony Center in Raleigh, 1971; Norwood Street in Wallace; King's Plaza in Raleigh, and the Main Office in Charlotte, 1972.

ENTERING THE NEW DECADE

The year 1970 marked the end of the economic expansion of the Soaring Sixties and the advent of the first recession of any real consequence in over a decade. During the latter half of the 1960s, the Federal Reserve imposed increasing restraints in an attempt to curb inflationary tendencies and to cool the overheating economy.

The restrictive monetary policy and its resultant tight money and high interest rates affected all areas of the nation's economy to some extent. The prime interest rate was forced to a high 81/2% early in 1970 through the combined pressures of consumer spending, business spending and the Vietnam War, and consumer demand for credit reached an all-time high. By the end of the year, however, the prime rate had dropped, credit demands had eased and the general economy was a bit sluggish. The lack of an overall demand for funds during 1972 in the money center banks kept bank rates down and affected earnings. The stage was being set for the economic crunch that was to come.

A CENTURY OF SERVICE

In the 1971 Annual Report, Mr. Satchwell reported to the shareholders, "It is difficult to dwell upon the results of a single year in the life of an institution which has been in existence 100 years. The basic foundation for the bank was set by its founder, Alpheus Branch, a man of great character. I consider myself fortunate indeed to have the privilege of serving as president of this fine old institution which, though mindful of its heritage, is young in outlook and is seeking to serve more effectively an ever-widening area of the state and nation."

GROWTH BY VIRTUE OF EXCELLENCE

Mr. Satchwell commented in 1973, "Branch Bank's whole philosophy is geared to healthy progress. We want no part of hasty construction, bigness just for the sake of bigness, growth with no sense of direction, but rather we subscribe to the idea of growth by virtue of excellence."

The bank's deliberate and steady growth during Mr. Satchwell's presidency extended into every significant area of activity.

The bank's total resources increased 135.6% during this nine-year period, going from $145,804,677 to $343,566,569. Loans rose from $53,332,013 to $200,835,488, an increase of 276.6%. The number of shareholders more than doubled, going from 1,080 to 2,357.

The number of banking locations increased from 35 in 25 Eastern North Carolina cities and towns to 60 locations in 35 cities and towns spread over much of the state.

Branch Bank also had redesigned its Management Development Program by this time after having received criticism from some of its young recruits. Satchwell asked Jack Mitchell to set up a more sophisticated training program. Mitchell had identified an easy-to-understand way to graphically illustrate two different types of loans, each with its own specifics with respect to maturity and repayment. Case studies were also being tested with this new method of teaching credit concepts. Mitchell began to test pieces of the new training program on a fairly new employee named John Allison, who was assigned to the Credit department.

Allison embraced the new training methods and suggested many improvements, Mitchell said. By June 1971, the four-month training program had been created. Allison was supervising the day-to-day operations of the Management Development Program in 1974.

THE ECONOMIC ENVIRONMENT OF THE 1970s

It has been said that the period from 1952 until 1966 was one of economic stability despite the three moderate recessions that had occurred. The nation's inflation problem developed between 1966 and 1970 during the time of the escalating Vietnam War when there was too much spending in relation to the quantity of goods and services being produced.[4] The so-called "guns and butter" policy with no tax increase to dampen domestic spending added fuel to the flame.

The stress that was developing within our economic system became apparent when inflation went from below 5% in 1972 to over 10% in the 1974-75 period.[5] Interest rates reached an unprecedented fever pitch in 1974; the worst unemployment in two generations followed; bankruptcies in banking, real estate, insurance and retailing reached a scale not experienced since the early 1930s; automobile sales in 1974 sustained one of the sharpest declines ever recorded; and the housing industry was especially hard hit.[6]

The year 1975 brought hopes for a brighter future. The inflation rate dropped to about 6% and allowed for a reversal of the Federal Reserve's tight money policy, which had been pursued for three years. A cut in withholding taxes and income tax rebates helped retail sales to revive, and from that point on, all economic indicators pointed toward recovery. Somehow, national economic catastrophe had been averted.

The two-year span from 1976 to 1978 was tranquil by comparison with the preceding years. Unemployment declined gradually, and the business world seemed to be recovering. Then, the consumer price index began to climb, first taking little steps, then giant steps, and inflation surged again.[7]

To keep the rate of inflation down to acceptable levels, the Federal Reserve shifted from an expansive monetary policy to a restrictive one late in 1978. Double-digit inflation since the beginning of 1979 pointed to continued monetary restraint.

During the first part of 1979, personal spending was advancing at about a 5% rate and the savings rate dropped to about 5% of disposable personal income.[8] The sharp rise in installment credit demands despite soaring interest rates caused prudent bankers to reassess their credit policies to avoid the overextension of credit. Later that year, the prime interest rate reached a record 15%, peaking at the end of the following year at 21 1/2%.

The challenge to the business community seemed to be finding ways to increase profitability to a point where it kept ahead of the seemingly inevitable inflation spiral without continually raising prices, which only fed inflation. Increased productivity and increased investment to replace outmoded plants and equipment would go a long way in solving the problem.

THORNE GREGORY ELECTED PRESIDENT

At the April 1972 meeting of the Board of Directors, Thorne Gregory was named president-elect to succeed Mr. Satchwell at the end of the year. Mr. Gregory was serving as senior vice president in charge of the Raleigh office, and the early announcement gave ample time for him to move to Wilson and work with Mr. Satchwell for several months to effect a smooth transition.

When Mr. Gregory became president on January 1, 1973, the nation was in a period of no growth, the prelude to recession. The growing inflation was creating an imbalance between expenses and profits, and competition in the banking industry had stiffened considerably.

The population per banking office in North Carolina declined from 10,169 in 1960 to 3,778 in 1972. While offering more convenience to customers, the added number of locations serving a fewer number of people increased competition among banks and was very expensive in terms of physical facilities.

Mr. Gregory said, "How do we react to the problems of decreasing profitability and increasing competitive pressure? We have done two things: We have streamlined and strengthened the management of the bank, and we have developed a long-range plan—a guide to the bank's future. I feel that this structure will allow us to create a dynamic environment which is so vitally necessary to attract and retain truly good people."[9]

In his first address to the shareholders, Mr. Gregory pointed out the dramatic changes that had occurred in the banking industry during the past decade. He said that there was a definite trend toward larger banks; the holding company concept was becoming popular; non-par banking was a thing of the past; costs were rising rapidly; and there existed a great demand for additional services. The manner in which Mr. Gregory faced each of these problems and the way he guided the bank through the deep recession yet to come proved him to be a worthy successor to the exceptional leadership the bank has had since its beginning.

EARLY TRAINING

Mr. Gregory's father, Fletcher H. Gregory, was one of the organizers of the Bank of Halifax which opened in 1906. After graduation from the University of North Carolina and four years as a pilot and instructor in the Air Force, Mr. Gregory joined the staff of the Bank of Halifax in 1956.

When the bank merged with BB&T in 1968, Mr. Gregory was elected a vice president and member of the board. He worked in the Wilson Office prior to his transfer to Raleigh, where he was promoted to senior vice president and later named officer in charge.

Mr. Gregory's five terms as a member of the North Carolina House of Representatives where he held key posts on numerous committees, his later graduation from banking and management schools, together with his thorough knowledge of banking, all combined to make him an adroit and perceptive leader. Mr. Gregory was especially skillful at recognizing and melding the talents of key personnel.

MR. GREGORY'S TENURE

The nine years that Mr. Gregory served as president constituted a dynamic period of profitability and growth in the bank's history. Assets increased from $343,566,569 to $1,133,584,000 or 303%. The number of shareholders grew by 45%, the number of offices by 49% and the number of cities serviced by 55%. This outstanding record of accomplishment stands as a lasting testimonial to Mr. Gregory's leadership.

The day Mr. Gregory became president, North Carolina's law prohibiting non-par banking went into effect. Other states had passed similar laws, and the result was a gradual reduction of correspondent bank balances. In spite of these losses, the bank's deposits continued to increase. These funds were replaced with deposits from corporations, firms and individuals by active solicitation and by increased emphasis upon serving the credit needs of customers.

MERGERS AND NEW OFFICES

The four mergers that occurred during Mr. Gregory's tenure broadened the bank's marketing area, primarily in the Piedmont area of the state.

The Bank of Matthews merged into BB&T on June 30, 1976, adding one office in the town of Matthews. The Citizens Bank of Warrenton, with two offices in Warrenton, merged on December 20, 1976. Headquarters for the Edgecombe Bank and Trust Company, which merged on October 20, 1980, were in Tarboro. Other offices were in Fountain, Farmville and Oak City, adding six offices in four communities.

Independence National Bank, which merged on October 5, 1981, operated 29 offices in 17 cities and towns, all in Gaston, Rutherford and Cleveland counties. This merger provided an important industrial-based economic balance to the predominantly agricultural character of the bank's traditional markets.

These mergers were important because they added 38 offices in 23 new cities and towns and accounted for approximately $383,000,000 additional assets. However, this increase in assets was less than 50% of the total growth that occurred during those years, the majority being in normal, internal growth.

In addition to offices acquired through mergers, the bank opened 27 new offices, seven of which were de novo. All of BB&T's offices with opening dates are listed in the Appendix.

BRANCH CORPORATION

Branch Corporation, a one-bank holding company, came into existence on July 1, 1974. Shareholders of Branch Banking and Trust Company exchanged each of their $5.00 par value shares for two shares of Branch Corporation with a par value of $2.50 each. The shareholders own Branch Corporation, which in turn owns Branch Banking and Trust Company. Thorne Gregory was named chairman and chief executive officer of Branch Corporation, and Albert S. Wylie was named president and chief administrative officer, a position he held until his retirement on September 2, 1981.

Plato Pearson, Jr., had been president of Independence National Bank prior to the merger with BB&T. On November 17, 1981, he was elected president of Branch Corporation, a position he held until his retirement on December 31, 1983.

The holding company structure equips the bank to move in any direction permitted by the regulatory authorities, allowing greater flexibility from an organizational viewpoint.

NCBA PRESIDENT

At the association's annual meeting in 1981, Mr. Gregory was elected president of the North Carolina Bankers Association, one of the highest honors that can be bestowed upon a banker in our state. He was serving as president at the time of his death.

MR. GREGORY'S DEATH

While jogging near his home on February 13, 1982, Mr. Gregory had a massive heart attack and died instantly. He was at the height of his career at the age of 53, and his death shocked and grieved the many friends he had made in banking, government and through numerous civic and church activities. ■

CHAPTER X

BB&T
1982-1992

The death of an experienced, widely respected and far-sighted leader can present a huge challenge to even the most stable of organizations. Ironically, BB&T would face such a loss twice during the 1980s. In each case, however, the bank would recover from its misfortune. In fact, despite the two tragedies that marred the decade, BB&T experienced a period of unprecedented growth and expansion during the 1980s.

Mr. Gregory's death seemed to come at a particularly bad time for BB&T. A recession that began in 1981 tightened its grip in 1982 and was followed by a period of "stop and go" recovery.[1] In the following years, government deregulation and deficit spending of a kind previously unknown helped feed an expansion that lasted for the rest of the decade.

United States stock markets rode this unprecedented period of growth until the Dow Jones Industrial Average reached an all-time high of 2,733.42 on Aug. 25, 1987. On Oct. 19, 1987, the Dow fell an unheard of 508 points in a crash many likened to the 1929 market disaster that marked the beginning of the Great Depression.[2]

Despite some dire predictions, however, the "Black Monday" crash of 1987 and smaller disturbances in the following two years failed to reverse the expansion and the economy continued to grow, albeit at a slower rate, into 1990.

MR. LOWE NAMED PRESIDENT

Three days after the sudden death of Mr. Gregory, the Board of Directors elected L. Vincent Lowe, Jr., president and chief executive officer of BB&T. He was also named chairman and chief executive officer of Branch Corporation.

Mr. Lowe grew up in Chadbourn, where his father and grandfather were bankers. After graduation from the University of North Carolina at Chapel Hill and military service in the U.S. Army, Mr. Lowe joined BB&T's Management Development Program in 1961.

He later became manager in Wallace and then in New Bern before returning to Wilson in 1970. He served as manager of the Bank Administration Division before being named senior executive vice president and chief operating officer.

As Mr. Lowe accepted the position left vacant by the death of his good friend Thorne Gregory, BB&T faced a critical period. The financial services industry was changing rapidly. Government regulations were repealed and competition increased. In an address to shareholders after his first full year as president, Mr. Lowe said BB&T must "analyze the environment in which we compete, evaluate our strengths and weaknesses, and establish realistic objectives and strategies. We have a great deal of confidence in our ability to plan for the future."[3]

To help draw these future plans, Mr. Lowe brought together a group of the best managers in the bank. His foresight in assembling a strong management team was destined to pay big dividends in the ensuing years.

GROWTH BRINGS CHANGES

On March 17, 1987, Garland Scott Tucker, Jr., announced his retirement as chairman of the BB&T Board of Directors. Mr. Tucker, a member of the board since 1954, had been appointed chairman on August 21, 1979. In announcing his retirement, Mr. Tucker said the office of chairman had grown to the point that the position required the attention of a full-time officer of the bank. The board immediately appointed Mr. Lowe as its new chairman.

One month later, on Mr. Lowe's recommendation, the board promoted John A. Allison IV to president of BB&T and Henry G. Williamson, Jr., to vice chairman of the bank. The Branch Corporation Board of Directors voted Mr. Williamson president of the corporation and Mr. Allison vice-chairman.

A Charlotte native, Mr. Allison joined the bank's Management Development Program in 1971 after receiving his bachelor's degree from the University of North Carolina at Chapel Hill. In 1972, he was named manager of Financial Analysis and, subsequently, manager of the Loan Officer Development Program. From 1973 to 1980, he served as a regional loan administrator. He was named manager of Business Loan Administration in 1980 and selected in 1983 as manager of the Banking Division (later expanded and renamed the Banking Group).

A native of Cerro Gordo, Mr. Williamson earned his bachelor's degree and master's degree from East Carolina University, graduating magna cum laude.

He joined the Management Development Program in 1972 and later served in the Fayetteville and Tarboro offices. He was a regional loan officer and manager of Bank Operations and Human Resources. He was named manager of the Administrative Group in 1983.

BB&T FINANCIAL CORPORATION

In May 1988, North Carolina's Secretary of State approved an amendment to the Branch Corporation charter changing the firm's name to BB&T Financial Corporation. The shareholders had approved the proposed amendment on April 26, 1988.

The new name would smooth the corporation's transformation into a multi-faceted financial services holding company.

"BB&T Financial Corporation is a name which allows us to retain our familiar logo and effectively continue our advertising and marketing efforts," Mr. Lowe said.

MR. LOWE'S DEATH

L. Vincent Lowe, Jr., chairman of the board of directors and chief executive officer, collapsed and died of a heart attack July 7, 1989, while playing tennis during a family vacation at Atlantic Beach, N.C.

Ironically, Mr. Lowe, who was 53 at the time of his death, had assumed BB&T's top position in 1982 after his predecessor Thorne Gregory died of a heart attack at the same age while jogging.

Meeting in emergency session on July 11, the board of directors for both BB&T and BB&T Financial Corporation named John A. Allison IV the new chairman and chief executive officer.

Raymond A. Jones, Jr., chairman of the executive committee, said the board acted unanimously in expressing support for the management team Mr. Lowe had assembled during his tenure. "We are confident they will continue the policies he initiated and, under John Allison's capable leadership, maintain the strong growth and progress we have experienced."

The BB&T board named Henry G. Williamson, Jr., the bank's new president. He continued in his position as president of the corporation.

In addition, the bank and corporation boards promoted the three other members of the executive management team to senior executive vice presidents. The three were Kelly S. King, manager of the North Carolina Banking Network; W. Kendall Chalk, manager of Loan Administration; and Scott E. Reed, chief financial officer.

On January 29, 1991, the bank and corporation boards named Mr. Williamson chief operating officer of the bank and chief operating officer and president of the corporation. Mr. King was promoted to president of BB&T. A Zebulon native, Mr. King received his undergraduate and master's degrees from East Carolina University, graduating magna cum laude.

BB&T Executive Management Team, 2000
(left to right) standing: W. Ken Chalk, Robert E. Greene, Kelly S. King, Morris D. Marley, Scott E. Reed; seated: Sherry A. Kellett, John A. Allison IV, Henry G. Williamson, Jr.

He joined the bank's Management Training Program in 1972 and served in management positions in Statesville, Charlotte, Wilson and Raleigh before being named manager of the Metropolitan Region in 1981. Under Mr. King's leadership, the region was reorganized as the Central Region in 1985. In 1987, Mr. King was named manager of Branch Administration and in 1988, manager of BB&T's North Carolina banking network.

GROWTH IN THE 1980s

Under the guidance of Mr. Lowe and his management team, BB&T experienced an unparalleled period of growth through expansion of existing asset bases and through mergers and de novo expansions. At the end of 1981, the bank held total assets of $1.13 billion and operated 121 offices in 64 cities and towns in North Carolina. On December 31, 1989, BB&T Financial Corporation controlled assets in excess of $4.8 billion and operated 191 offices in 105 cities and towns in North and South Carolina.

INTERSTATE BANKING

When the United States Supreme Court handed down a ruling in June 1985 that established states' rights to enter into reciprocal interstate banking agreements, BB&T was ready. Applying a carefully conceived strategy, BB&T identified the most desirable markets in neighboring southeastern states and began negotiations with potential merger candidates.

These negotiations bore fruit on December 29, 1986, when Branch Corporation announced that a merger agreement had been signed with Community Bancorporation, Inc., a bank holding company headquartered in Greenville, S.C. Acquisition of the 13 offices of Community Bank was completed in July 1987. Assuming its new name the following February, BB&T of South Carolina included branches in the communities of Greenville, Spartanburg, Easley, Greer, Seneca and Simpsonville.

BB&T of South Carolina opened a new branch in Mauldin in late 1988. In 1990, the bank opened an office in Columbia and relocated the Spartanburg main office into a new 17-story tower. The following year, BB&T's Greenville main office became the anchor tenant in the city's tallest office tower, the 25-story Daniel Building.

EXPANSIONS IN NORTH CAROLINA

The 1980s also saw BB&T expand significantly its markets in North Carolina. An important goal was to strengthen the bank's position in the major metropolitan markets in the state.

A merger agreement with City National Bank on June 6, 1983, gave BB&T five offices in Charlotte and added approximately $78 million to the bank's assets. This merger greatly expanded BB&T's customer base in the Charlotte metropolitan area and increased our ability to compete throughout Mecklenburg County. It also provided the bank with a larger main office in a more desirable location.

Carolina BanCorp, Inc., and its subsidiaries, the Carolina Bank and the Bank of Alamance, merged with BB&T on July 2, 1984, adding approximately $300 million in assets and 28 offices in 21 cities and towns. The merger gave the bank an expanded market in the Sandhills area of the state. BB&T's assets exceeded $2 billion for the first time.

BB&T used de novo expansion to enter the expanding Triad Area formed by Greensboro, Winston-Salem and High Point. In 1983, we opened an office in Greensboro and added an office in Winston-Salem the following year. The main office in High Point opened in August of 1988, followed by another office in High Point in October 1989.

The Triad expansion has benefited greatly from the bank's decision to open branch offices inside Kroger stores, making BB&T the first major North Carolina bank to open offices in large supermarkets. In 1986, two branch offices opened in Kroger stores in Greensboro and one in Winston-Salem. Another Kroger location in Greensboro and two more in Winston-Salem were in operation by early 1988. The bank's first office in High Point opened in a Kroger store in 1987. The Kroger partnership was expanded into the Triangle Region with the opening of two offices in Raleigh Kroger stores in late 1989.

Entry into Asheville and Hickory was achieved in 1986 when BB&T purchased six offices from First Union National Bank in the aftermath of its merger with Northwestern Bank. This acquisition also gave us offices in Maggie Valley, Fletcher, Longview and Old Fort. Main offices were added in Hickory in March 1988 and in Asheville in December 1988. Another Asheville office was opened in March 1989.

BB&T opened its first office in Wilmington in 1984 and constructed a new main office in the coastal city in 1987. Our first offices in Durham and Rocky Mount opened in 1985, and branch offices were added in both cities in 1987.

From 1982 to early 1990, BB&T also opened new main offices in Plymouth, New Bern, Morehead City, Roanoke Rapids, Burlington, Knightdale and Cary.

The Charlotte market strengthened with the opening of several new branches, including another new concept for BB&T—offices located within retirement communities. The first opened in February 1989 in the Plantation Estates retirement home in the Charlotte suburb of Matthews. The second opened in July 1989 in the Methodist Home retirement community in Charlotte.

Other Charlotte area openings included a new Queen City office in early 1990 and a branch in nearby Pineville in late 1986.

In 1985, a rapidly growing BB&T occupied a new seven-story office tower adjacent to its existing Home Office building in Wilson. Also completed in Wilson during the early 1980s were a 72,000 square-foot Operations Center housing data processing and bank operations, and a complex for warehousing, purchasing and printing functions.

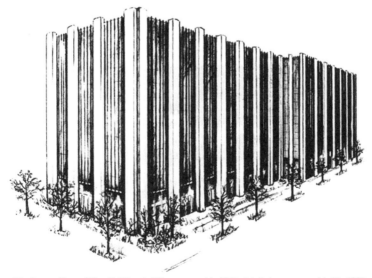

The former Home Office Building in Wilson opened in 1971. A twin tower was added in 1985.

OUR MISSION

Mr. Lowe and his executive management team directed a rewriting of the corporation's Mission Statement in 1984 to reemphasize our commitment to being a customer-driven organization. The Mission Statement emphasizes our belief that the customer is our reason for being. By achieving the goal of providing high quality financial problem-solving services through highly skilled, self-motivated people, we will achieve profitability and maximize the return shareholders earn on their investment.

SERVICES

The changing banking environment of the 1980s saw banks offer myriad new and different products and services. With an eye toward the future, BB&T enhanced and updated the options available to its customers as their needs changed and as new legislation created more opportunities.

Significant new services introduced during the period included Cash Management, International Services, the OMNI and Elite banking packages for upscale customers, the UVEST (Brokerage Service*), Individual Retirement Accounts, Basic Checking, the Money Market Investment Account and BB&T Club 50, an enhanced service package for customers aged 50 and older.

From its introduction in 1977, our network of BB&T 24 automated teller machines grew to 97 throughout the state by the end of 1989. Through participation in the nationwide PLUS SYSTEM®** and the regional RelaySM network, customers were given access to their accounts at any of several thousand ATMs throughout the United States.

Customers who use our automated teller machines received an added benefit in early 1990 with the introduction of BB&T 24 Inquiry, a service that allows customers with a BB&T 24 card to get account information by telephone 24 hours a day.

* UVEST is a registered trademark of Mercantile Securities Corporation.
** Owned by PLUS SYSTEMS, Inc.

SPECIAL SERVICES

Complementing BB&T's well-rounded program of commercial banking services are the Trust, Insurance, Mortgage Loan and Travel Departments.

The Trust Department, the second oldest in the state, opened in 1907 and has since become one of the major divisions of the bank. As BB&T entered the 1990s, trust accounts administered by the department were helping the fourth and fifth generation descendants of the original beneficiaries. The division's activities encompass personal trusts, corporate trusts, employee benefit and farm management services.

In late 1984, the State of North Carolina awarded BB&T the contract for its 401(k) plan, a tax-deferred supplemental retirement option available to more than 255,000 state and local government employees whose total annual earnings exceeded $4.5 billion. The plan became operational in 1985. In late 1989, BB&T won the right to continue to administer the plan, one of the largest of its kind in the country, through 1996. This and other 401(k) contracts expose the bank to a large block of new customers creating excellent retail cross-selling opportunities. BB&T Trust personnel in Raleigh and Charlotte administer 401(k) plans.

The bank's Insurance Department began in 1922, primarily writing fire insurance. In 1987, the bank set a goal of establishing the premier independent insurance agency in the state. That same year, BB&T purchased an established agency in Asheville to complement its existing property and casualty, and life insurance, agencies in Raleigh and Wilson.

Since then, the Insurance Department has opened new local agencies in Wilson, Gastonia, Greenville and Trenton and acquired existing agencies in Charlotte, Hickory and High Point.

The Life Insurance Department underwent two name changes during 1989, changing to the Life and Group Health Department, then to Life and Financial Planning.

The Travel Department, established in 1963, prepares itineraries and arranges domestic and foreign accommodations for an ever-increasing number of vacation and business travelers.

The Mortgage Loan Department, established in 1923, makes and services residential and income property mortgage loans. By the end of 1989, the department had grown to encompass more than 110 mortgage lending personnel across the state who serviced more than 14,000 loans representing an investment of almost $1 billion in the people of North Carolina.

A NEW WAY TO DO BUSINESS

In late 1988, BB&T implemented a dramatic shift in strategy touted by its executive management as a "new way we do business."

Concerned that the bank was approaching a size that would make it difficult to continue to offer quick, responsive customer service, BB&T's management reorganized the North Carolina branching network.

The creation of 10 distinct regions, each headed by a regional president, was intended to decentralize decision making and shift authority to the branch level. Customer contact individuals in each region were given more authority to make independent judgments on how best to serve their unique markets. Home office functions were redesigned to better respond to decisions made at the regional level.

Each regional president was given the authority traditionally reserved for presidents of smaller "community banks." In turn, the presidents were asked to turn over more authority to the customer contact employees within their region.

Customers and employees alike responded favorably to the reorganization. Analysts praised BB&T for its new strategy and said the reorganization would position the bank to do well during the 1990s, a period expected to be rife with consolidation and fiscal uncertainty.

The 10 regional presidents named in November 1988 were: Jesse W. "Rip" Howard, Coastal Region; Max S. Crowe, Eastern Region; David E. Crowder, Mecklenburg Region; Russell W. "Danny" Daniels, Jr., Neuse River Region; David R. Clark, Northwestern Region; Stephen L. Medlin, Roanoke Valley Region; L. Allen White, Sandhills Region; Michael K. Goodman, Triad Region; R. Lee Youngblood, Triangle Region; and W. Alex Hall, Western Region.

CAPITAL PLANNING

BB&T's rapid growth created the need for additional capital at a time when new banking regulations called for more capital reserves. In 1985, following an analysis of the bank's future capital needs, the bank found market conditions favorable, and the corporation issued $34.5 million in 20-year convertible debentures, the first long-term debt issued by the corporation or the bank.

Later that year, the corporation issued $50 million in floating rate notes. The proceeds provided a substantial amount of additional funds to support our asset base and to provide for ongoing operations.

In 1985 and 1986, a sale and leaseback transaction involving 18 buildings netted the bank $32.4 million. In essence, this arrangement converted nonearning assets into earning assets and boosted net income.

Additional sources of capital were developed through a dividend reinvestment plan that enables shareholders to reinvest their dividends into shares of BB&T Financial Corporation stock. BB&T employees may elect to purchase the corporation's stock through the employee thrift plan.

A formalized Investor Relations department was established to make the corporation better known in the financial community.

THRIFT ACQUISITIONS

On Aug. 9, 1989, President George Bush signed into law a massive piece of reform legislation designed to relieve problems caused by troubled savings and loan institutions. While estimates of the cost of this "bailout" ranged from $200 billion to more than $500 billion, and although many saw the need for further legislation to finally solve the problems, the new law had an immediate impact on BB&T.

Anticipating the passage of the Financial Institutions Reform, Recovery and Enforcement Act (FIRREA), BB&T began negotiations with a number of thrift institutions in the late 1980s. Expecting the new legislation to permit banks to acquire healthy savings and loan organizations and convert them to banking offices, BB&T became one of the first banks in the country to negotiate such an arrangement.

On May 24, 1989, BB&T announced its intention to acquire Carolina Bancorp, parent company of First Federal of the Carolinas, a $316 million thrift. The First Federal acquisition would give BB&T four new offices in High Point, Greensboro, Jamestown and Thomasville and add more than 100 employees.

On Oct. 23, 1989, BB&T announced an agreement to acquire a sound savings and loans institution headquartered in Greenville. First Federal Savings Bank of Pitt County included offices in Greenville, Ayden, Farmville and Grifton, $141 million in assets and some 40 employees.

Gate City Federal Savings and Loan was the third thrift to agree to join BB&T and the largest to that point. Announced on March 27, 1990, the addition would give BB&T eight offices in Greensboro and one each in Eden, Madison and Reidsville. The $461 million thrift with 140 employees was one of the soundest mutual savings and loans in North Carolina.

On April 30, 1990, BB&T announced a merger agreement with Home Savings and Loan Association, a $243 million thrift with 50 employees and five offices in Durham, Chapel Hill and Roxboro.

On July 19, 1990, Albemarle Savings and Loan Association became the fifth thrift to agree to join BB&T. Headquartered in Elizabeth City with a branch in Kitty Hawk, Albemarle added $91 million in assets and 30 employees.

More than a year of negotiations followed these first five announcements. Then, on August 27, 1991, BB&T announced an agreement with People's Federal Savings Bank, a $106 million organization with two offices and 33 employees in Thomasville.

First Fincorp, the parent company of First Financial Savings Bank, became the seventh thrift to agree to join BB&T on April 21, 1992. With 10 offices located across North Carolina, the $347 million thrift strengthened BB&T in its home location of Kinston and in Goldsboro, Morehead City and Winston-Salem. It added the new markets of Elkin, King, LaGrange, Lewisville and Mount Airy and 175 new employees.

On May 13, 1992, BB&T signed a nonbinding agreement with Security Financial Holding Company, parent of Security Federal Savings Bank. Under the agreement, BB&T would acquire the $340 million thrift and its nine offices, including seven in Durham, one in Chapel Hill and one in Creedmoor.

The merger also would add 93 new employees.

Through early 1992, BB&T had reached agreements that would allow it to grow by adding some 48 offices, $2 billion in assets and 650 valuable new employees to BB&T in North Carolina.

Under provisions of FIRREA, BB&T began merging the newest members of the BB&T family into the North Carolina banking network after August 1991.

The stage was set for the monumental merger-of-equals with Southern National Corporation. ■

Allison, Orr Agree To Merger

It all started with a simple telephone call in 1994, an early July phone call to John Allison from Glenn Orr. Orr suggested the chief executives meet to discuss an in-market "merger of equals" between the bank he led, Southern National, and Allison's BB&T.

Allison needed no persuading. He, like Orr, had been thinking a lot about mergers. Interstate banking, which would allow one bank to buy another almost anywhere in the United States, was a year off. Allison knew the legislation would be inviting to big out-of-state banks looking for a foothold in the lucrative Carolinas banking market. By merging, Allison and Orr acknowledged, they could create an institution better positioned to ward off potential acquirers.

OMNI HOTEL IN RICHMOND

They agreed to meet for a preliminary talk on July 15, a Friday morning, at the Omni Hotel in Richmond, Va. Before they went any further, the two would see if they could agree on questions like what the bank would be called, where it would be based and, most important, who would run it. Allison would later say that, going into the meeting, he didn't know whether or not a second session would ever be held in light of the thorny questions they would tackle from the outset.

But the three-and-a-half-hour meeting went smoother than he expected. They picked Southern National for the corporation name because it traded on the New York Stock Exchange. They chose BB&T for the operating name because it had more branches than Southern National, saving money in signage costs. They chose Winston-Salem as the headquarters, home to Southern National and the fourth largest market in North Carolina.

ALLISON TO BE CEO, ORR TO RETIRE

Then they agreed Allison would become CEO of the new institution. Orr would retire. Orr would later tell *Business North Carolina* magazine, in a 1995 interview, that Allison was more of a "strategic thinker" than he was. He also said that Allison's participatory-management style would be well-suited to the new corporate culture. The new senior management team would include four managers each from BB&T and Southern National, while the new board of directors would be made up of 12 members, each from the company's existing boards.

On Tuesday, July 19, Allison boarded the BB&T company plane and flew to Myrtle Beach airport, about 30 miles south of Sunset Beach, where Orr was vacationing. Orr picked Allison up and headed south on U.S. 17. They rented a conference room at Litchfield Beach, an oceanfront resort, and met one-on-one for 15 hours, dressed in khakis and loafers in case anyone recognized them together. If word of the impending deal leaked, Allison and Orr feared, they might have to consider an offer from another bank, something they wanted to avoid.

On Thursday, Allison and Orr met again at Litchfield Beach for another 15-hour meeting. There were more phone calls on Friday and Saturday. On Sunday, July 24, Allison and Orr flew to Washington, D.C., where they met with lawyers and their investment bankers. They spent the next week preparing for upcoming board meetings in Wilson and in Southern National's hometown of Lumberton.

ANALYSTS PRAISE DEAL

By Aug. 1, both boards had approved the deal and the branches had been informed. Allison and Orr were ready to make the merger announcement in Winston-Salem, taking the media and the industry by surprise. Two weeks from the day they met in Richmond for their first meeting, Allison and Orr had closed a deal that analysts would praise as a model in the industry for mergers of equals.

The new corporation, with more than $18 billion in assets, could now afford to make investments in technology and expand its lines of business. With a higher market capitalization, it could better plan for future acquisitions.

On Nov. 18, 1994, BB&T announced that normal attrition and early retirement would significantly reduce the number of required personnel cuts resulting from the merger. Only five percent of the new work force would be laid off and BB&T promised to help those employees find new jobs through its Career Transitions Program. The program offered assistance in resume preparation, job-seeking skills, and the use of office space and mail services.

The successful conversion included a new practice that would be embraced for years to come. The Conversion Support team or "buddy system" called for a legion of BB&T employees to work side-by-side with fellow staffers joining BB&T through the merger.

With the practice still in use more than a decade later, the buddies include customer service representatives, relationship bankers, tellers and more, who volunteer to shadow new employees and calm their jitters. In many cases the buddies are away from their families day and night for two weeks until a conversion is completed. Often they are employees who have benefitted from having a buddy when they were part of the merger process and volunteer to return the favor.

On Dec. 15, 1994, BB&T and Southern National jointly announced that more than 90 percent of shareholders from each company had cast votes in support of the merger.

Positive results came quickly following completion of the merger on May 30, 1995. First-quarter earnings in 1996 produced returns well above most banks its size. Return on assets was 1.4 percent, meaning it earned $1.40 for every $100 of assets it had. Analysts began to upgrade their recommendations from "hold" to "buy" on the new Southern National stock. One year after the merger was completed, the new bank had created more than $800 million in additional shareholder wealth.

Ever the strategist, Allison immediately laid out a 10-year plan for stockholders and employees, a plan designed to maintain BB&T's position as an independent, high-performance company. Allison envisioned a BB&T that would cover the Southeast and Middle Atlantic, specializing in small-business lending and consumer-banking services. His plan, as he put it, was to build the best financial institution possible – "the best of the best."

Part of Allison's plan included committing to paper BB&T's guiding principles, including the vision, mission and values, philosophy, and other guiding principles. These were the basic tenets that had drawn so many to BB&T and provided a reason for their long tenure as BB&T employees.

MISSION STATEMENT

To help get it there, BB&T adopted several management philosophies, including the following mission statement: *To make the world a better place to live by*:

- Helping our CLIENTS achieve economic success and financial security;
- Creating a place where our EMPLOYEES can learn, grow and be fulfilled in their work;
- Making the COMMUNITIES in which we work better places to be; and thereby:
- Optimizing the long-term return to our SHAREHOLDERS, while providing a safe and sound investment.

BB&T'S PURPOSE

BB&T's stated purpose in 1997 read as follows: *Our ultimate purpose is to create superior, long-term, economic rewards to our owners (shareholders.)*

- However, we can only accomplish this purpose with excellent client relations as our clients are our source of revenues.
- To have excellent client relations we must have outstanding employees to serve our clients. To attract and retain outstanding employees, we must reward them financially and create an environment where they can learn and grow.
- Our economic results are significantly impacted by the success of our communities. The community's "quality of life" impacts its ability to attract industry for growth.
- Therefore, we manage our business as an integrated whole with the ultimate objective of rewarding owners (shareholders) for their investment while realizing that the cause of this result is quality client service. Excellent service will be delivered by motivated employees working as an integrated team. These results will be impacted by our capacity to contribute to the growth and well-being of the communities we serve.

BB&T'S VALUES

BB&T Values Statement: *Values are important at BB&T. Values are practical guides to action.*

- **Fact-based decision-making** (reality): What is, is. If we want it to be better, we must act within the context of the facts (reality.)

- **Reason** (objectivity): We will make logical decisions based on the facts and act on these decisions.

- **Independent thinking**: All employees are challenged to use their individual minds to their optimum to make rational decisions. In this context, each of us is responsible for what we do and who we are. In addition, creativity is strongly encouraged and only possible with independent thought.

- **Productivity**: We are committed to be producers of wealth and well-being by taking the actions necessary to accomplish our mission. The tangible evidence of our productivity is that we have allocated capital rationally through our lending and investment process and that we have provided needed services to our clients in an efficient manner resulting in superior profitability.

- **Honesty**: Being honest is simply being consistent with reality. To be dishonest is to be in conflict with reality and is, therefore, self-defeating.

- **Integrity**: Regardless of the short-term benefits, acting inconsistently with our principles is to our long-term detriment.

- **Justice** (fairness): Individuals should be evaluated and rewarded objectively (for better or worse) based on their contribution to accomplishing our mission and their adherence to our values.

- **Pride**: We must perform our work in such a manner as to be able to be justly proud of what we have accomplished.

- **Self-esteem** (self-motivation): We expect our employees to earn positive self-esteem from doing their work well. We want employees who have strong personal goals and who expect to be able to accomplish their goals within the context of our mission. A necessary attribute for self-esteem is self-motivation. We have a strong work ethic. We believe that you receive from your work in proportion to how much you contribute. If you do not want to work hard, work somewhere else.

- **Teamwork/Mutual Supportiveness**: While independent thought is critically important, our work is accomplished within teams. Each of us must consistently act to accomplish the agreed upon objectives of the team with respect for our fellow employees, while acting in a mutually supportive manner.

BB&T'S CONCEPTS

BB&T senior management also listed the following concepts to describe BB&T:

- **Client-driven** (Our clients are our partners. We try to create win/win relationships.)
- **Quality-oriented** (Quality must be built into the process.)
- **Efficient** ("Waste not, want not." Design efficiency into the system.)
- **Growing** both our business and our people (Grow or die.)
- **Continuous improvement** (Everything can be done better.)
- **Objective decision-making** (Fact-based and rational.)

BB&T MANAGEMENT STYLE

And, finally, senior management listed BB&T's management style and management concept:

Management style:

- Participative
- Team-oriented
- Fact-based
- Rational

Management concepts:

- Hire excellent people
- Train them well
- Give them an appropriate level of authority and responsibility
- Expect a high level of achievement
- Reward their performance

As 1999 drew to a near close, venerable BB&T was still the leading mortgage lender and originator in the Carolinas and trustee for North Carolina's 401(k) plan, the largest state government pension plan in the nation. It was proud to be the country's most small business-friendly bank and parent of the 12th largest bank-owned insurance agency in the nation.

Since the merger of equals, BB&T had doubled its asset size. It was a $40 billion bank by the third quarter of 1999, operating more than 600 banking offices in 17 regions.

WORLD STANDARD PERFORMANCE

Even as it grew, BB&T steadily climbed the ranks in key measures of banking performance such as profitability, efficiency and credit quality, landing it in the top 10 percent of U.S. bank holding companies.

The goal for 2000 would be to continue to make significant progress toward distinguishing itself among the nation's top performers – to be the best of the best.

The world standard.

In March 1999, *Business Week* magazine named BB&T the second highest performing bank in the United States. BB&T's original visionaries – Alpheus Branch and Thomas Jefferson Hadley – who in 1872 founded the bank that would become BB&T, could not have hoped for more. ■

Rapid Growth

With the vast growth in the Raleigh, N.C., area, BB&T moved its Raleigh headquarters to 434 Fayetteville St., the city's newest high-rise building, in 1991.

The five years following the 1994 merger-of-equals announcement were another rapid period of growth and prosperity for BB&T. By 1999, it had become the nation's 23rd largest bank–with more than $37 billion in assets. It was an exciting period of diversification as the venerable bank – the oldest in North Carolina–continued to expand its franchise and diversify its product line, securing a promising future in the evolving financial services industry.

UCB MERGER PROPELS BB&T TO NO. 1

BB&T announced a major merger agreement in late 1996 with Whiteville, N.C.-based United Carolina Bancshares. Of the several acquisitions to follow over the next three years, none would be bigger than the $985 million UCB deal. UCB's $4.4 billion in assets gave BB&T control of the largest share of deposits (20 percent) of any bank in North Carolina and the third largest share in South Carolina (11 percent.)

Analysts applauded the merger, pointing out that both banks had solid capital positions, excellent credit quality, strong branch networks and compatible corporate cultures. UCB Chairman and Chief Executive Officer Rhone Sasser pointed out that UCB customers would now be able to take advantage of BB&T's extensive line of products and services while continuing to do business with a bank where decisions would be locally made. Sasser would retire as chairman and chief executive and serve on BB&T's Board of Directors.

BB&T completed the conversion on Sept. 22, 1997, when 91 UCB banking offices opened as BB&T branches and 67 more were consolidated into existing locations across the Carolinas. BB&T, the former "farm bank," was now the 30th largest bank in the country, with more than $27 billion in assets and 486 offices across North Carolina, South Carolina and Virginia.

But it was only getting started.

NORTHWARD EXPANSION

An immediate corporate goal was to look to acquire banks with $250 million to $5 billion in assets, especially in Virginia. The first move toward building a statewide presence in Virginia was completed in July 1996, when the 21 offices of Virginia Beach-based Commerce Bank opened as branches of BB&T of Virginia.

The merger was seamless for Commerce customers as the Hampton Roads Region's largest community bank had actually been part of the BB&T family for 18 months prior to conversion.

The 20-member Commerce Bank Board of Directors became directors of the new BB&T of Virginia Board, with Commerce President and CEO Robert Aston as president of the Virginia bank. The Hampton Roads Region became the 15th region in the BB&T tri-state banking network. The regional system was set up in 1988 to give local bank officers as much authority as possible. It allowed presidents of each BB&T region to make loans of up to $2 million (or 95 percent of all loans) without having to get approval from corporate headquarters.

After the Commerce merger was completed, the bank announced an agreement to purchase Richmond, Va.-based Fidelity Financial Bankshares Corporation in a $59.4 million stock transaction. BB&T acquired Fidelity Financial's $328 million in assets and seven branches in the Richmond area, operated through its subsidiary, Fidelity Federal Savings Bank.

Fidelity Financial President Barry Crawford became the regional president of the new Richmond Region. The Fidelity Financial Board of Directors formed the Richmond Region Board and became directors of BB&T of Virginia.

The Fidelity Financial purchase was the first BB&T thrift acquisition since 1993, when the following were acquired: First Financial Savings Bank ($322 million in assets), Security Federal Savings Bank ($316 million),

Carolina Savings Bank ($142 million), Edenton Savings & Loan Association ($40 million), 1st Home Federal ($188 million), Citizens Savings Bank ($263 million), Mutual Savings Bank ($87 million), Old Stone Bank of N.C. ($537 million) and Citizens Savings Bank ($63 million).

These acquisitions were the result of a BB&T innovation called "merger-conversions," whereby a depositor-owned thrift would convert to stockholder-ownership and simultaneously merge with a big bank. It was hailed as a fairly inexpensive way to rapidly build market share.

BB&T was back on the Virginia acquisition trail in 1997, announcing in May that it would purchase Virginia First Financial Corporation, a Petersburg-based savings and loan, in a stock transaction valued then at $148 million.

The acquisition gave BB&T a foothold in the southern, central and southwestern regions of Virginia. BB&T acquired Virginia First's $817 million in assets, which included 24 banking offices and 12 mortgage loan production centers in Virginia and Maryland under Virginia First Mortgage. At the time of the merger, Virginia First had 432 employees.

ENTERING WASHINGTON, D.C. AND MARYLAND

The northward expansion continued in March 1998 when BB&T acquired Life Bancorp Inc. of Norfolk, Va., in a $359.2 million stock transaction. The acquisition gave BB&T the largest market share of deposits in the Southside Hampton Roads area, which included Norfolk, Virginia Beach, Chesapeake, Portsmouth and Suffolk.

Life Bancorp, with about $1.5 billion in assets, operated 20 full-service banking offices through its banking subsidiary, Life Savings, FSB. Its primary businesses were retail banking and mortgage banking. BB&T had about $3.5 billion in assets and $2.3 billion in deposits in Virginia following the merger

In December 1997, BB&T announced it would be moving into Washington, D.C., with the $170 million acquisition of Franklin Bancorporation Inc. Metropolitan Washington, with 5 million people, was ranked at the time as the fifth largest metropolitan statistical area in the nation.

Franklin Bancorporation, with about $659 million in assets when the deal was completed in July 1998, operated 10 full-service banking offices, six in the District of Columbia, one in Bethesda, Md., and three in Northern Virginia.

Robert Pincus, Franklin's president and CEO, was named president of the D.C.-metro region, the newest of BB&T's 17 autonomous regions. BB&T's decade-old regional system of operation allowed the bank to keep its traditional "community bank feeling" as it continued to grow.

In October 1998, BB&T completed its acquisition of Maryland Federal Bancorp Inc. The $239 million deal more than doubled BB&T's presence in metropolitan Washington, D.C. Maryland Federal, with about $1.2 billion in assets, operated 28 branches in five counties in the Maryland suburbs of Washington.

The acquisition moved BB&T from 21st to 11th in deposit size in metropolitan D.C. Continuing its push into the region, BB&T announced in August 1998 that it would buy MainStreet Financial Corp. of Martinsville, Va., for about $554 million in stock.

The acquisition significantly expanded the bank's presence in southwest and central Virginia while adding a handful of offices in the Washington area. With $2 billion in assets, MainStreet operated 46 banking offices in Virginia and three in Maryland.

The acquisition combined BB&T's autonomous approach to local decision making with the premier community banking franchise in Virginia. Martinsville became headquarters of BB&T's third Virginia region.

INTO GEORGIA, WEST VIRGINIA AND KENTUCKY

BB&T began 1999 with two major acquisition announcements in two days.

On Jan. 26 the bank announced it would acquire First Citizens Corporation of Newnan, Ga., in a $125.9 million stock transaction that would give BB&T its first entry into Georgia.

The acquisition would move BB&T into the metropolitan Atlanta area, a rapidly growing region with 3.14 million people. Atlanta was the largest metropolitan statistical area in the Southeast and a major financial center on the East Coast.

First Citizens, with $421 million in assets, operated 13 banking offices and one mortgage loan office in five metropolitan Atlanta counties.

BB&T now had a platform for future expansion in Georgia and the high-growth Atlanta area. First Citizens also provided a natural extension to the bank's Greenville and Spartanburg, S.C., presence.

The next day, BB&T announced it would acquire Mason-Dixon Bancshares of Westminster, Md. The $256.9 million stock transaction would double BB&T's presence in Maryland.

Mason-Dixon would increase BB&T's assets to about $2.4 billion in Maryland, where BB&T would rank eighth in market share. Mason-Dixon's branch network included 23 banking offices, 12 consumer finance offices and three mortgage loan offices. Its $1.1 billion franchise would extend BB&T's presence to economically strong markets in metropolitan Baltimore and central Maryland.

Less than a month after the Mason-Dixon announcement, BB&T announced it would buy Matewan BancShares Inc. of Williamson, W.Va., in a stock swap valued at $157.9 million. The transaction not only moved BB&T into two new states – West Virginia and Kentucky – it also strengthened the bank's growing Virginia franchise. Matewan BancShares, with $676 million in assets, operated 22 banking offices and one mortgage loan office in southwestern Virginia, southern West Virginia and eastern Kentucky.

The Matewan, Mason-Dixon and First Citizens acquisitions – all scheduled for completion in the third quarter of 1999 – would give BB&T banking offices in seven states and Washington, D.C.

On April 28, BB&T announced it would acquire First Liberty Financial Corp. of Macon, Ga., in a $500 million stock swap that would give BB&T its second Georgia bank.

First Liberty Financial, with $1.7 billion in assets, operated 39 banking offices and 13 consumer finance offices in Macon and Savannah, Ga., and neighboring areas. Its principal subsidiaries include First Liberty Mortgage Corp. and OFC Capital Corp., an equipment leasing subsidiary.

The acquisition, scheduled for completion in the fourth quarter of 1999, would extend BB&T's presence from northern Maryland to southern Georgia.

On July 28, BB&T announced it would acquire Premier Banc-shares of Atlanta in a $624.1 million stock swap giving BB&T its third Georgia bank and the sixth largest share of deposits in metropolitan Atlanta.

Premier Bancshares, with $2 billion in assets, operated 32 banking offices in Atlanta and North Georgia and 10 mortgage banking offices through a subsidiary, Premier Lending.

As if announcing or consummating six bank acquisitions (Mason-Dixon, First Citizens, Matewan BankShares, First Liberty, Premier Bancshares and Hardwick Holding) in one year were not enough in 1999, BB&T announced one more in December – First Banking Company of Southeast Georgia. The deal was a $124.2 million stock swap and BB&T's sixth acquisition in Georgia that year. BB&T began 1999 with no bank offices in Georgia, but when all the pending acquisitions were completed, BB&T was Georgia's eighth-largest bank with more than $5 billion in assets.

INVESTMENT BANKING

BB&T completed the acquisition of its first investment banking firm, Richmond, Va.-based Craigie Inc., in October 1997. The 68-year-old brokerage house specialized in the origination, trading and distribution of fixed-income securities and equity products in both the public and private capital markets.

With $80 million in assets and $23 million in annual sales, the firm's niche was in writing debt equity, especially in helping municipalities raise money for such projects as building bridges and schools.

Gaining quick entry into the investment banking arena was a historic step for BB&T, a move analysts lauded as an excellent diversification strategy. The Federal Reserve cleared the way for the deal in late 1996 by relaxing the Depression-era law known as Glass-Steagall that separated commercial and investment banking. For most of the 20th century, banks weren't allowed to be in the securities business because of potential conflicts between commercial lending and investment banking.

Though the Fed began allowing banks to do securities underwriting in 1989, it capped banks' corporate underwriting at 10 percent of the revenue in their securities affiliates. In late 1996, the Fed loosened the cap to 25 percent, expanding the volume of investment banking that commercial banks could do. That paved the way for banks to begin courting larger brokerage firms.

In August 1998, BB&T announced it would acquire regional brokerage and investment banking firm Scott & Stringfellow in a $131 million stock transaction. Established in 1893, the Richmond, Va.-based full-service brokerage managed more than $10 billion in assets for its clients.

On the brokerage side, Scott & Stringfellow, through its 32-office network in the Carolinas, Virginia and West Virginia, assisted clients with their personal investment portfolios by recommending stocks or other securities. It also served institutional investors, big mutual fund companies such as T. Rowe Price, Fidelity and Oppenheimer.

On the investment banking side, Scott & Stringfellow helped companies raise money through the capital markets and worked with firms interested in mergers or acquisitions. About one-third of the firm's investment banking business came from underwriting public equity offerings.

Craigie would now fold into Scott & Stringfellow to form an autonomous investment banking subsidiary of BB&T. The combination provided BB&T customers access to both the equity and debt markets. BB&T was truly on its way to becoming a "one-stop shopping" financial center.

INSURANCE ACQUISITIONS

Reece

BB&T Insurance Services is one of the company's great success stories. BB&T had been in the insurance business since 1922, but by the late '80s to early '90s it was losing money.

In 1990, Henry Williamson approached Wade Reece, then area manager in Gastonia, N.C., about creating synergies between the bank and the insurance business to make the insurance side profitable again.

"Henry called and wanted me to meet with him," Reece said. "So I met with him and he told me about his idea that I should move into insurance. I said, 'Henry, that's kind of a crazy idea. I think you know this, but I want to be honest. I don't know anything about insurance except to trust my agent.' Henry smiled and said, 'Good start.'"

BB&T Insurance Services, the largest bank-owned insurance agency in the East, expanded its roster of agencies in 1995 when it added six agencies in North Carolina: Boyette Insurance and Realty Corporation of Fayetteville, Poole Insurance Agency of Greensboro, Webb Insurance Agency of Statesville, Frank Wilson Agency of Rocky Mount, the Proctor-Owen Insurance Agency of Roanoke Rapids and the Enfield Insurance Agency of Enfield.

Raleigh, N.C.-based BB&T Insurance Services would later acquire agencies in South Carolina and Virginia: James R. Lingle Agency of Florence, S.C., William Goldsmith Agency and C. Dan Joyner Insurance Agency, both of Greenville, S.C., Boyle-Vaughan Associates of Columbia, S.C., and Virginia agencies DeJarnette & Paul, Inc. of Richmond and W.C. Brown Insurance of Rocky Mount.

BB&T purchased its first title insurance agency with the 1997 acquisition of Consumers Title Company of Fayetteville, N.C.

In March 1998, BB&T Insurance Services added McPhail, Bray, Murphy & Allen of Charlotte. In December it acquired Blue Ridge Burke of Winston-Salem and Mount Airy.

BB&T Insurance Services gained entry into metropolitan Atlanta in March 1999 by acquiring the Huffines-Russell agency. It then added three more Virginia-based agencies over the next two months – Old Dominion Insurance Services, E.W. Barger & Company and G.C. Wright Co. Inc.

The bank's insurance arm entered metropolitan Washington, D.C., in April by acquiring Givens & Williams Inc. of Fairfax, Va. Also in April, BB&T Insurance Services acquired the book of business of Greensboro, N.C.-based Mays Insurance and acquired James River Title Agency Inc., an independent title insurance agency in Richmond, Va.

In July, BB&T Insurance Services boosted its coastal presence in North Carolina by acquiring Beam, Cooper, Gainey & Associates to bring its agency roster to 24 in North Carolina, 15 in Virginia, three in South Carolina and one in Georgia.

It was the largest independent agency in the Carolinas and the 12th largest in the country.

SALES AND MARKETING STRATEGIES

One of BB&T's most important strategies following the merger of equals was to implement an aggressive sales culture - a system known as "Cohen Brown" – that quickly became a way of life for branch employees. Each branch would hold a meeting every Monday morning to set specific Cohen Brown goals for the week. Customer service representatives, for example, might call 20 customers that week to pitch checking accounts. By Wednesday, there would be a progress report, and by Friday, results from each branch and region would be keyed in and sent to headquarters in Winston-Salem.

The Cohen Brown aggressive sales process—and the employees who learned and practiced it—was credited with doubling in 18 months the number of BB&T customers who used five or more banking services. Many of those customers were former savings and loan customers who were accustomed to savings accounts, home loans and little else. As BB&T customers, they could now explore investment, insurance and trust options from one of the most efficient and profitable banks in the country.

Cohen Brown complemented BB&T's multi-million dollar marketing campaign, launched in 1996 to heighten awareness of the BB&T brand name following the merger of equals. In keeping with that effort, the corporation changed its name from Southern National to BB&T Corporation in May 1997, tying the holding company name to the company's banking subsidiaries in the Carolinas and Virginia.

Beginning May 19, shares of BB&T Corporation were traded on the New York Stock Exchange under the new symbol, BBK (which replaced SNB.)

In December, Standard & Poor's Financial Information Services added BB&T Corporation to the S&P 500 Index, a leading indicator of stock market performance among major U.S. companies.

BB&T changed its trading symbol to BBT on Jan. 4, 1999.

VENTURE CAPITAL INVESTMENTS

In January 1996, BB&T announced it would spend $50 million to add new product lines by buying stock in small Southeastern companies specializing in bank-related technology and services.

BB&T wanted to invest in—or buy—software firms, consumer finance companies, specialty investment management firms, specialty finance companies, etc. The goal was to obtain at least a 25 percent return on its investments.

When the announcement was made, the bank had already made venture-capital investments in Farr Associates Inc., a leadership consulting firm based in Greensboro, N.C. (now High Point, N.C.); and Nexus Software Inc. of Raleigh, N.C., a company that produces networking software for mid-size to large banks.

At the time of the announcement, banks of BB&T's size rarely invested in companies other than banks. Federal law required banking companies to get permission from the Federal Reserve before buying more than 5 percent of another company's stock. But because BB&T is regulated by the state of North Carolina, it didn't have the same restrictions.

By June 19, the $50 million acquisition plan began to pick up momentum with an announcement that BB&T had purchased the assets of MedStar Leasing Co., an Asheville, N.C.-based business specializing in the leasing of medical equipment to doctors, clinics and hospitals. BB&T purchased the company from St. Joseph's Hospital in Asheville.

With about $10 million in receivables, MedStar would join Charlotte-based BB&T Leasing Corporation with its eight offices in the Carolinas. Before the MedStar deal, BB&T Leasing Corporation specialized primarily in business leases for vehicles and general equipment. Now it could expand into a new line of business, a goal the bank would meet time and again in the late 1990s.

In August 1996, BB&T became a majority shareholder of AutoBase Information Systems, a Charlotte-based company that specialized in matching car buyers and sellers. AutoBase later changed its name to Auto Allies.

BB&T's automotive dealership customers would now be able to take advantage of Auto Allies' Vehicle Listing System (VLS), which provided information on the availability of different makes and models of new and used cars. The VLS system would also lower marketing costs for dealers.

The Auto Allies deal came just five months after BB&T announced it would buy Regional Acceptance, a 24-year-old Greenville, N.C.-based company specializing in higher-risk used auto loans.

The $182 million deal would allow BB&T to expand its customer base while receiving a premium for Regional's higher risk loans–loans banks had traditionally shunned.

With 27 branch offices and 150 employees in North Carolina, South Carolina, Tennessee and Virginia, Regional was seen as another venture capital acquisition for BB&T. Williams R. Stallings, a former N.C. Entrepreneur of the Year, would continue his role as chairman and chief executive officer of Regional Acceptance, which would operate as a BB&T subsidiary after the deal.

With Regional, Auto Allies and BB&T's existing auto sales finance operation, the corporation could now provide its customers with an integrated finance and marketing program designed to benefit both automobile dealers and auto consumers.

On Jan. 23, 1997, BB&T gained entry into yet another new line of business when it announced plans to purchase Refloat Inc. of Mount Airy, N.C., and its principal subsidiary, Sheffield Financial Corp., a finance company in nearby Clemmons, which catered to lawn care businesses across the country. Sheffield built its business by lending to landscaping firms buying high-end lawn mowers and other outdoor power equipment and providing direct credit for customers of lawn and garden equipment dealers.

Less than two weeks after the Refloat/Sheffield announcement, BB&T announced it would purchase Phillips Factors Corporation and its subsidiaries, Phillips Financial Corporation and Phillips Acceptance Corporation, all of High Point, N.C. Founded in 1979, Phillips Factors' niche was buying and managing account receivables, primarily in the furniture, textiles, home furnishings-related and temporary staffing industries.

In March 1998, BB&T's venture capital investments effort picked up steam again when the bank formed BB&T Capital Partners LLC, a subsidiary that would invest between $1 million and $5 million in established small businesses and middle-market growth companies in the South.

BB&T Capital Partners initially was capitalized with more than $40 million to invest in rapidly growing companies with strong management teams.

In May, BB&T announced the acquisition of Dealers Credit Inc. (DCI), a national finance company based in Menomonee Falls, Wisc., that specialized in lawn care equipment loans. It would operate within Sheffield.

DCI, founded in 1991, had more than 11,000 commercial, agricultural, consumer and municipal customers across the country. The addition increased Sheffield Financial's customer base to more than 30,000 nationwide.

DCI's expertise with retail dealers and Sheffield's focus on manufacturers would combine to make BB&T a national leader in lawn care equipment financing.

Then, in June, BB&T announced it had acquired W.E. Stanley & Company Inc., an actuarial and employee benefits consulting firm located in Greensboro, N.C., and its two subsidiaries, Corporate Compensation Plans of North Carolina Inc. and Corporate Services Inc.

W.E. Stanley, the largest actuarial, consulting and administration firm in the Carolinas, primarily managed retirement plans for companies of all sizes. Founded in 1954, W.E. Stanley served more than 700 clients in the eastern half of the United States, with a concentration in the Carolinas, Virginia, Maryland and Tennessee.

W.E. Stanley's specialties included the design and administration of pension plans; defined contribution plans, such as 401(k), profit sharing and ESOPs; health and welfare plans; "cafeteria" benefit plans; and executive compensation plans.

With the addition of W.E. Stanley, BB&T more than doubled the number of plans it administered to more than 1,250.

ALTERNATIVE DELIVERY

As BB&T continued to look outside the corporation for opportunities to grow and diversify its product line, it also looked within for new and innovative ways to improve customer service.

On March 14, 1996, the bank announced it had created a new division dedicated to non-traditional banking. The Alternative Delivery System's three initial objectives were to create a 24-hour telephone banking center to be staffed by live operators, a personal computer-based home banking system and an expanded network of automated teller machines (ATMs) located at "off-site" locations such as convenience stores and fast food restaurants.

On Dec. 16, BB&T's customized personal computer banking system made its debut. With BB&T OnLine, bank customers could now pay bills, transfer money, and get balance and transaction information–at the click of a button–24 hours a day, seven days a week.

The bill-paying service enabled customers to pay anyone–businesses or individuals–electronically. Payments could vary in amount, such as electric or telephone bills, or customers could set up fixed recurring payments for monthly bills such as mortgage or auto loans. If the payee was not equipped to accept electronic payments, BB&T would cut a check and mail the bill. Either way, BB&T OnLine eliminated the customer's need for checks, envelopes, postage and trips to the mailbox. The system also was set up to let customers check account balances, review transactions and transfer money among eligible accounts. For the first time, customers could manage their finances without ever having to leave home.

BB&T then launched an on-line banking system designed for small business customers in April 1997. With BB&T Business OnLine, one of the Southeast's first on-line banking programs for small businesses, companies could pay bills and monitor their accounts at any time, using a toll-free direct line rather than an Internet connection.

It was a significant new product for a bank that already was the leading small business lender in the Carolinas and one that would be named the top "small business friendly" bank in the country a year later.

The Alternative Delivery news continued in September 1997 when BB&T opened BB&T Direct, its new 24-hour call center. BB&T retail customers now had two options when questions about their accounts came up: the voice-response activated BB&T Phone 24 system or the operator-staffed call center. Both provided account balances, check clearance information and answers to other common banking inquiries.

The call center also offered customers the opportunity to ask more specific questions and carry out banking transactions by telephone. BB&T Direct was headquartered in Whiteville, N.C., honoring a merger agreement BB&T made with Whiteville-based UCB.

BB&T also closed out 1999 with record earnings that totaled $659.1 million, or $1.97 per diluted share (excluding nonrecurring charges primarily associated with mergers and acquisitions). Net income was up 17.5 percent. However, bank stocks took a tumble from fear that interest rates would rise and some banks were expected to report poor results. BB&T's stock, which had been around $40 per share, sunk to the mid 20s at year's end. ∎

CHAPTER XIII

New Millennium, New Challenges, New Opportunities

BB&T, like the rest of the world, began making plans for the new millennium well in advance of the actual date change. This planning began with the realization that many computer systems had a date-related programming glitch that could create a multitude of problems with how the bank conducted day-to-day business.

Computer programmers and information technology professionals far and wide waded into a sea of computer codes to ensure systems did not mistake the two-digit "00" code to represent the year 1900 rather than the year 2000. Imagine, for example, getting a computer-generated past-due notice from your local library on Jan. 15, 2000, for more than $9,000 – a quarter a day since Jan. 1, 1900.

In hindsight, what became known as Y2K was the first of many uncharted territories that BB&T and its employees would navigate in just the first decade of the new millennium. Through it all, BB&T's management maintained that whether the new millennium issued in new technologies, a more global economy or anything else, some things would remain constant – BB&T's vision, mission, values and client-driven strategy.

THE Y2K CHALLENGE

Discussions about the widespread Y2K preparations were referenced often in daily news coverage. The "millennium bug" was not limited to computers. All kinds of devices with electronic components, including elevators and bank vaults, had embedded microprocessors that referenced dates.

1997 1998 **1999**

BB&T spent three years and approximately $30 million preparing for the 2000 date change

Today, Y2K is often referenced as a "non-event." Few incidents related to the date change actually occurred and that's exactly what those engrossed in the project worked so hard to achieve.

"There was a tremendous amount of hype around Y2K and nobody knew what to expect because none of us had ever been through it before," said Leon Wilson, who had served as Bank Operations manager since 1982 and was promoted to senior executive vice president and a member of BB&T's Executive Management team in December 1999. "It turned out to be a non-event, but that's because we did what we needed to do before Y2K to evaluate and remediate all our networks and systems. It was like any risk management process – who knows what may have happened if we had not done all that work. I think there would have been serious ramifications if we had just ignored it, but you had to work hard to separate the truth from the fiction. BB&T did a pretty good job of that. Obviously, we came through it without any damage."

Evaluating all the codes that supported BB&T's systems was no small task. BB&T conducted an initial inventory of systems several years prior to the date change. At one point, more than 100 employees occupied an entire building dedicated solely to the Y2K effort. The employee newsletter, *The Insider*, noted that BB&T spent approximately $30 million preparing for the new millennium.

"It was an enormous amount of work to check every single line of code to make sure that anywhere a date existed, the system could not only accept the new date but also process it," said Barbara Duck, who was a member of the Operations Division at the time and became senior executive vice president and member of BB&T's Executive Management team in 2003. "You wouldn't think this would be that difficult but there were a lot of different coding languages, and our systems were very interwoven and reliant on each other to pass data. It was a very, very complicated process."

Contingency plans, were created to include operating a Corporate Command Center on Dec. 31 and for the next several days.

"We were all there when the date changed, and everyone was holding their breath," Duck said. "In true BB&T fashion, we had a very organized, thoughtful, methodical process. When the end of the day came and went without any notable interruptions, everyone in IT and Operations took a lot of pride in their accomplishments. It was exactly what we wanted."

ONE VALLEY MAKES BB&T NO. 1 IN WEST VIRGINIA

Until July 2000, BB&T's acquisition strategy had been to target franchises in the $500 million to $3 billion range and build a presence in one market before moving into other markets in that same state.

The strategy changed when BB&T acquired Charleston, W.Va.-based One Valley Bancorp. One Valley, BB&T's largest merger since the Southern

BB&T's merger with One Valley gave the bank the No. 1 market share in West Virginia.

National merger of equals in 1995, catapulted BB&T from No. 10 in market share in West Virginia to No. 1.

"One Valley was a company we'd been calling on for a long time because they were a super cultural fit," Allison said. "They also had the No. 1 market share in West Virginia, and Holmes Morrison, their chief executive officer, was a guy BB&T could have hired and trained ourselves. We knew we could run a very efficient profitable operation with the One Valley merger, which would help finance new growth markets."

The $1.13 billion transaction boosted BB&T from controlling 1.6 percent of West Virginia deposits to nearly 18 percent. The deal also strengthened BB&T's No. 6 position in Virginia and gave it entry into 10 new Virginia markets. One Valley increased BB&T's trust assets by 40 percent and enhanced its mortgage loan operation with the addition of a successful mortgage loan origination and servicing platform.

"From a conversion perspective, One Valley was very exciting," Barbara Duck said. "It was our largest conversion other than the merger of equals. Even more exciting was to get to the other side of the conversion and really see the family that came out of it."

The 9/11 attacks shocked the nation and made BB&T aware of risk exposure
not previously considered.

SEPTEMBER 11, 2001

On Sept. 11, 2001, Americans took a cumulative gasp as unthinkable terrorist attacks occurred on our homeland.

- Around 9 a.m. hijacked American Airlines Flight 11 crashed into the North Tower of the World Trade Center in New York City. Minutes later, United Airlines Flight 175 crashed into the South Tower.
- At approximately 9:30 a.m. hijacked American Airlines Flight 77 crashed into the Pentagon in Washington, D.C.
- At nearly 1:30 p.m. United Airlines announced the crash of hijacked Flight 175 southeast of Pittsburgh, Pa.

The terrorist plan was to disrupt the country's financial markets, Allison recalled. Fortunately, they didn't know about the New York Clearinghouse's backup systems, he said.

The attacks set off shockwaves across America and throughout the world. The son of one of BB&T's regional presidents died in the World Trade Center. Other BB&T employees recalled exiting the building or watching the astonishing events from nearby offices or sidewalks.

Several members of Executive Management remember their meeting being interrupted with the news.

"We quickly assessed what it could mean to BB&T," Leon Wilson said. "We didn't know if this was a one-time event or something that was going to happen every day. It opened up a whole different level of disaster and contingency planning and made us aware of risk exposure we hadn't thought much about prior to those events."

BB&T contributed $250,000 to the American Red Cross followed by a $25,000 donation to the September 11th Fund in honor of the BB&T employees and their families who were directly affected by the tragedy.

The New York Stock Exchange, American Stock Exchange and NASDAQ were closed for four business days. When the markets reopened stocks dropped 684 points. The real estate market in Washington, D.C., also shuddered for several months.

Years later the effects are still felt in the banking industry. In response to the attacks, Congress passed the USA Patriot Act of 2001, which included a number of anti-terrorism measures largely dealing with electronic surveillance and law enforcement access to records. Additionally, Title III of the Patriot Act required financial institutions to track and prevent money-laundering and terrorist financing activities.

The act, which strengthened the 33-year-old Bank Secrecy Act, required financial institutions to be compliant by Oct. 1, 2003.

In observance of the 10-year anniversary of the tragedy, BB&T Chairman and CEO Kelly King reflected on the day:

> *"When the first building was hit, I immediately focused on my son who often travels to New York City. Fortunately, he was in Charlotte, N.C. But he had worked in one of the towers the previous summer and knew a lot of people who lost their lives.*
>
> *One of our regional presidents lost his son in the tower that day. I attended a ceremony some weeks later where our regional president and his wife still held out hope for his recovery. We all prayed together.*
>
> *For the first day and the next several weeks, our team was really worried about a financial system collapse and the horrific effects such would create. It was a scary time.*
>
> *In December of that same year, I took my 16-year-old daughter to New York City and visited the World Trade Center site. Even 90 days later, smoke still came up from the deep dark hole where the buildings had once stood tall.*
>
> *As I held my daughter, I cried. 9/11 was tragic, and I still agonize over the loss of so many lives. Yet, as I stood there with my daughter, I felt a strong sense of hope for her life and our country. I am proud to be an American."*

Daniel Hoff, a BB&T Wealth Management advisor in Sarasota, Fla., recalled escaping from the South Tower that fateful day.

> *"I was on the 61st floor of the South Tower of the World Trade Center for my second day of a three-week training program. I didn't see when American Airlines Flight 11 struck the North Tower, but I saw it ablaze with thousands of documents pouring from it. The impact cracked the window glass on the South Tower. As we walked down the stairwell there was an announcement that the South Tower was secure. I remember thinking, 'Thank God, we're safe.' Maybe five or 10 seconds later, the second plane struck. We didn't know what happened. We felt the building shake and smoke blew up from beneath while jet fuel poured down the HVAC, but we thought it could have been the result of damage to the North Tower. We counted each floor we made it down and came out through the mall underneath the World Trade Center. I was so happy to have the blue sky above me. The thing I'll never forget is this beautiful sky and then the horrible sight. My first thought was, 'This can't be happening.' While some wanted to stay and see what was happening, I wanted to leave and began walking toward midtown. At some point, I remember looking back and seeing that the South Tower had collapsed. The first person I called was my wife. We still have the message I left to tell her I was OK. Every day I'm more appreciative. I think of everything I've done in the past 10 years, and I think it could have been stolen from me. We don't want to let people forget. Part of me will always be in that stairwell."*

First Virginia was the largest bank holding company based in the state.

FIRST VIRGINIA

It took less than a month for BB&T to announce its first merger in 2003. With the acquisition of First Virginia Banks Inc., BB&T became the nation's 11th largest financial institution. The new BB&T had approximately $91 billion in assets and more than 1,300 offices in 11 states and Washington, D.C. It increased BB&T's market share in Virginia from fifth to second; to No. 7 in Maryland, which ranked third in the nation for household wealth, and to No. 10 in Tennessee. It also expanded BB&T's footprint in metro Washington, D.C.

"Burney Warren (then manager of acquisitions and venture capital investments) and I had been calling on First Virginia to try to talk them into selling to us once a quarter for 15 years," Allison said. "First Virginia had a great market and the largest retail distribution system in Virginia, and it was squeaky clean in terms of credit risk."

Falls Church, Va.-based First Virginia was the largest bank holding company based in the state. First Virginia had $11.2 billion in assets and, like BB&T, operated a community banking structure that emphasized client service within its eight community banks and 364 branch offices.

Allison said combining two of the highest performing banks in the country positioned BB&T for long-term growth.

"If the leaders stay, the employees stay, and if the employees stay, you get the potential to really grow the business," said Chris Henson, then president of Georgia operations and the Atlanta-based community bank region. "That's what we had with First Virginia."

SUCCESSION PLANNING

While BB&T had emphasized leadership development and succession planning prior to the deaths of Thorne Gregory and Vincent Lowe, their deaths at such early ages made the necessity for it exceedingly clear.

The BB&T Executive Management team that formed in the early 90s following Lowe's death continued to develop and formalize the existing Management Development Program (later known as the Leadership Development Program), created the BB&T Banking School in 1997 and emphasized succession planning in preparation for their retirements. The early 2000s were a time of transition when several such plans came to fruition.

"It's always important for every organization to do proper succession planning, not only at the CEO level but throughout the organization," Allison said. "I think it's a moral obligation that we have to be sure the company is prepared to go on after we leave."

King, who was BB&T Corporation president and the manager of BB&T's North Carolina Banking network at the time of Lowe's death, credits such foresight for the successful transition of Allison taking the helm as CEO.

"Had we not had succession planning in place it would have been really bad," King said. "BB&T's succession planning ensured a smooth transition in the event of Mr. Lowe's untimely death. Then we began orchestrating the next levels of, not only CEO succession, but succession for the whole executive team."

Six members of the Executive Management team – Allison, King, Williamson, Reed, Chalk and Greene – had all joined BB&T at about the same time. They were all in their 40s when Allison became CEO. In a few years, they began to realize that most of them would retire within a five- or six-year period. And, during the mergers and acquisitions they had seen many cases when a company was being sold, at least in part, due to little or no succession planning.

"We could identify and begin to bring several new members on to Executive Management because we had made a 30-plus year investment in leadership development," Allison said. "BB&T invests a lot more on leadership development than any of our competitors. It's been a long-term strategy. We knew we had people who were proven leaders, who had been given many different opportunities and who understood our culture, vision, mission and values."

BB&T began bringing these new leaders on in a staged process. Leon Wilson, who had served as Bank Operations manager since 1982 was promoted to senior executive vice president and a member of the Executive Management team in December 1999.

Sherry Kellett, the first female to join BB&T's Executive Management team in 1998, announced that she would retire as corporate controller in August 2003.

In December that same year, Chief Operating Officer Henry Williamson Jr. announced he would retire in June 2004.

Barbara Duck, manager of the Production Management Group responsible for merger conversions, and Steve Wiggs, director of the newly created Wealth Management Division, were named to the Executive Management team in August 2003.

Executive Management Team as of 2012, from top left: King, Bible, Brown, Duck, Goodirch, Greene, Henson, Starnes, Wiggs, Wilson

In 2004, King succeeded Williamson and two new members joined BB&T's Executive Management team. Ricky Brown, president of the Washington, D.C.-based community bank region, who assumed King's role, and Chris Henson was named assistant chief financial officer.

When Chief Financial Officer Scott Reed retired in June 2005, Henson was named as his successor. Clarke Starnes and Donna Goodrich both joined Executive Management in December 2006.

Daryl Bible, who was recruited from U.S. Bank, joined the Executive Management in January 2008, as chief financial officer. And, Chalk retired as chief credit officer in September 2008 and was succeeded by Starnes.

"This gave each of them the opportunity to work with the existing Executive Management team before our group began to retire," King said. "It worked really well. John, as CEO, continued to have very forthright conversations with the board about the strengths and weaknesses of each team member, who would be ready to succeed him immediately and what members may need to do to be ready. I think the organization should feel very good about this. I think it's a testament to our organization." ■

Building Business

In the two years that followed the First Virginia merger, BB&T took a self-imposed hiatus from bank mergers and acquisitions and concentrated on organic growth. Two factors contributed to that decision – "digesting" the recent string of mergers and acquisitions, as Allison was known for saying, and the dramatic increase in premiums that competitors began paying for such deals.

"Prices really got out of line," Henson recalled. "A number of acquisitions in BB&T markets occurred where BB&T was the logical buyer, but those banks were acquired by other companies. For example, Fifth Third Bank paid a 50-percent premium for First Charter in Charlotte, N.C. A couple of other deals like that were made for banks in Alabama and Florida. Any time the market heats up to double what you should be paying it's time to exercise discipline. John Allison and Kelly King really led this disciplined approach and it was absolutely the right thing to do."

Such discipline and adherence to BB&T's values have been the key to BB&T's success, but it prompted many to pin a conservative label on the company.

"During my career, we went from $4.5 billion in assets to $136.5 billion," Allison said. "That's a highly aggressive company. People confuse principled with conservative. What we are is rational and principled, and there's a big difference."

BB&T evaluated acquisitions using a trusted financial model and made decisions based on the results.

"It was a very tempting time. The way financial models work, you can change all the assumptions and make anything look good," Allison said. "But we didn't deviate from our model and a lot of the companies that did those deals ended up failing. We think some of the best deals we made are the ones we didn't do. In some ways, they were the hardest. It's tempting to rationalize, but we were very disciplined."

ORGANIC GROWTH

Putting acquisitions aside, BB&T focused on organic growth by adding new financial centers, strengthening existing client relationships and winning new business from bank prospects. The company also expanded specific growth areas, such as Insurance, Wealth Management, Corporate Banking and Lending.

From 2004-2006, BB&T added approximately 70 de novo financial centers, located primarily in North Carolina, Georgia and Florida.

BB&T had long identified itself as the bank that provides the best value to its customers by delivering top-tier service that became known as the Perfect Client Experience. Such service supports organic growth and is delivered in conjunction with a process that began in early 1999 and has become Integrated Relationship Management (IRM). The idea is simple – as BB&T helps its clients become more successful, it also will become more successful.

"Organic growth is basic blocking and tackling, making sure we serve our clients so well that they do more business with us," said President of Community Banking Ricky Brown. "It includes an active calling process to ensure we understand our clients' needs and refer them across lines of business to help them achieve their financial goals. It's about growing new relationships through a persistent sales effort. It also includes opening branches in markets where we don't have one."

BB&T opened one of its new prototype financial centers on
Robinhood Road, Winston-Salem, N.C., in 2008.

A former managing director of Lehman Brothers wrote that among the more than 1,000 financial institutions he had worked with, BB&T was the first to demonstrate such a collaborative approach. He indicated that he first called BB&T to discuss refinancing his residence, a transaction that closed in 10 days. A few days later, he received a call from another employee who had learned that he was interested in expanding his business and wanted to see if BB&T could help him in that process. Then a relationship banker got a commitment from him to open an account when she called to discuss his personal banking needs and to tell him he qualified for a home equity line of credit.

This IRM strategy followed the 1999 Gramm-Leach-Bliley Act, which expanded the powers of banks and bank holding companies to sell financial products or services. The act made shopping for financial products more convenient for clients as it cleared the way for banks, securities firms and insurance companies to own each other and cross-sell products and services. The act repealed the Glass-Steagall Act, which in 1933 prohibited banks from selling securities.

IRM expanded the use of the core bank's sales process to Financial Services divisions. To support the IRM strategy, BB&T introduced new software that helped make it possible for the company's entire sales force to provide sales leads across lines of business.

"We evaluated how we were really doing in terms of organic growth," Brown said. "We checked to see if our sales metrics were right, what kind of results we were getting from our client calls and if our coaching and inspection processes were where they should be. Our consultative, trusted advisor model came out of that work."

The process revealed strengths and weaknesses that BB&T used to improve and create a competitive advantage.

"It has served BB&T well," Brown said. "We've seen client service quality scores increase year after year."

WEALTH MANAGEMENT

In 2000, BB&T created a Private Financial Services team to serve the financial needs of its affluent clients. The goal was to make an array of financial services accessible to these busy clients through a single contact.

In 2003, BB&T introduced its Wealth Management Division, which combined Private Financial Services and Personal Trust into one group under the direction of Chief Marketing Officer Steve Wiggs. The decision was made after research showed the wealth segment had grown more than 25 percent in the past five years and was expected to continue at that pace for the next decade.

Using a team concept, Wealth Management advisors coordinated the delivery of a whole gamut of products and services – banking, investments, tax planning, insurance and estate planning. The Wealth Management advisors were supported by specialists from Asset Management, Investment Services, Scott & Stringfellow and Insurance Services.

Wealth prospects were identified as high-net-worth individuals and families who seek a higher level of proactive service and objective financial advice.

"Over the years, we've developed strong relationships by lending to commercial clients as they have grown their business and wealth," Wiggs said. "Some of our best wealth clients and prospects are commercial clients, who were getting their wealth needs met elsewhere because we weren't as focused on developing and promoting these services as we needed to be. The good news is we're now getting great recognition and commentary from our client base about how we're doing in the wealth business."

Executive oversight for the Wealth Management Division transitioned to Henson in 2009, and by 2011 the business had grown considerably.

Wealth clients were segmented into four groups – emerging affluent, Private Financial Services, Wealth Management and the Sterling Capital Private Client Group.

"Proactively targeting wealth and large commercial clients has worked well for BB&T," Henson said. "These areas along with Insurance and Lending have helped us diversify our revenue base."

CAPITAL MARKETS/CORPORATE BANKING

In 2000, BB&T aligned its Corporate Banking Division with Capital Markets to create a unified group to serve all public, large private and nonprofit organizations. Doing so allowed the division to provide an approach to raising capital that integrated corporate banking with public and private debt and equity solutions. To capitalize on the expertise in Capital Markets, Corporate Banking aligned its relationship management nationally by industry.

In the fall of 2009, BB&T began to expand the Capital Markets Division to capitalize on competitors weakened by the Great Recession and diversify BB&T's portfolio by growing commercial and industrial loans. As a result, BB&T Capital Markets has become a formidable player in the middle-market and large-corporate companies using the financial strength of BB&T and the expertise of Capital Markets to deliver best-in-class service and build long-term relationships with clients.

INSURANCE

By 2010, BB&T Insurance Services had grown to the sixth largest broker in the U.S. and seventh in the world. The business unit, which employs more than 4,000 people, has grown from generating approximately $6 million in revenue in 1990 to more than $1 billion in 2010.

"Our evolution has been similar to the bank's," said Wade Reece, chairman and CEO. "While we once were more of a generalist providing small business, agrarian-type coverage, we have diversified and broadened our services. We're in specializations today that we only dreamed of a few years ago."

While the evolution of BB&T Insurance Services may mirror the bank's, the acquisition activity during this period was considerably more aggressive. Areas of specialization came largely through the approximately 60 acquisitions BB&T Insurance Services has completed since 1999. These deals gave BB&T Insurance a wholesale brokerage, large account capabilities, and expertise in utilities, health care, education, transportation, marine transportation and more. Milestone acquisitions included Cooney Rikard & Curtin (CRC) Inc. in 2002 and McGriff Seibels & Williams in 2004.

In 2011, Birmingham, Ala.-based CRC was the second largest wholesale property and casualty insurance broker in the nation. The deal created opportunities for BB&T Insurance Services as well as provided diversity of operations in the insurance distribution business.

CRC provides insurance for specialty and high-risk industries. Dry cleaners, for example, have difficult environmental risk management issues. A tremendous need existed at BB&T Insurance and among other CRC clients for these types of insurance. To address this need, Southern Cross in Jackson, Miss., and TAPCO in Burlington, N.C., were acquired and became Southern Cross TAPCO.

McGriff Seibels & Williams was the 13th largest retail broker in the U.S. when it was bought by BB&T. It specialized in a number of industries, such as transportation, utilities and energy, and it had large account capabilities. The addition of McGriff also created IRM potential among BB&T's Corporate Banking and Capital Markets team.

"We were building out our large account capabilities and McGriff accelerated that process," Reece said. "McGriff gave us a national retail platform. It was a significant deal in the industry. Strategically, it was a great combination, and it's been a very successful acquisition."

In 2008 alone BB&T Insurance completed 11 acquisitions, including San Diego-based UnionBanc Insurance Services, expanding its operations in California, the No. 1 state for insurance premiums in the country. The 2008 acquisitions fueled a record year for business in 2009. But the economy plunged in 2009 resulting in a sole acquisition of Oswald Trippe and Company Inc. of Fort Myers, Fla. The following year was void of acquisitions, but in the third quarter of 2011 BB&T Insurance announced three acquisitions within two months – Precept Group and Liberty Benefit Insurance Services, both in California, and Atlantic Risk Management Corp. of Columbia, Md.

LENDING

In 2009, Executive Management reevaluated BB&T's corporate structure regarding revenue growth and risk management. We needed to align revenue areas better and build a new risk management organization. As a result, the Lending and Marketing group was formed with Marketing as a revenue support area for all BB&T lines of business.

By design, the Lending group has developed over time to meet the vast lending needs of our clients. Whether commercial-oriented, with a national strategy of stand-alone lending locations, or retail-oriented, with a BB&T footprint strategy via the branching network, our lending businesses provide strategic product and geographic diversification for BB&T's loan portfolio.

In 2011, the Lending group included:

- **Commercial Finance** – consisting of Asset Based Lending, Factoring, Supply Chain Finance and Mortgage Warehouse Lending
- **Dealer Financial Services** – consisting of Dealer Finance, Regional Acceptance, Recreational Lending, Floor Plan Financing and the Portfolio Acquisition group
- **Equipment Finance**
- **Governmental Finance**
- **Grandbridge Real Estate Capital**
- **Lendmark Financial Services**
- **Mortgage** – consisting of Retail Lending and Correspondent Lending
- **Premium Finance** – consisting of AFCO, CAFO and PrimeRate
- **Retail Lending** – consisting of Direct Retail Lending and BankCard Services
- **Sheffield Financial**

OTHER MARKETS

Hispanic Outreach

In 2001 BB&T formed the Hispanic Initiative Task Force to identify how BB&T could support this growing population. While Hispanics were identified as the largest growing minority group with an estimated buying power of $40 billion, most were under banked and brand loyal. The team gathered and analyzed research from more than 100 sources and conducted focus groups of Hispanics throughout BB&T's footprint.

Jack Snow, president of Sheffield Financial, led the company into the new market of powersports in 2009, financing the likes of Polaris snowmobiles.

In 2003, Executive Management approved the task force recommendations, which included an aggressive business development strategy. A brightly colored logo was developed with a new tagline, "el banco que nos apoya," which means "the bank that supports us." Initially, BB&T tried a direct translation of "You can tell we want your business," the corporate tagline at the time. However, the literal translation in Spanish was "We're going to take your business away" – hardly an effective message when trying to build trust and convey welcome.

A series of educational tapes that featured a character named "Bibi" was created to help serve the growing Hispanic population.

A series of cassette tapes that featured a character named "Bibi" (after the two Bs in BB&T) was created to provide insight into life in America. The stories, written to resemble the soap operas popular among many Hispanics, were broadly distributed and well received. The first bilingual Help Desk was also created in Whiteville, N.C., in 2003.

BB&T identified the need for and created a product called EnvioFacil to address one of the population's top banking needs – a money transfer product that allows clients to transfer funds to anywhere in the world for free. In August 2009, BB&T launched a Hispanic version of its website called BB&T Vecino, which means "neighbor," to assist the Hispanic population with their banking needs.

In September 2007, BB&T opened its first financial center in a heavily Salvadorean pocket of Northern Virginia. By 2009, the branch ranked among the top 10 in deposit account growth. BB&T now operates more than 262 multicultural financial centers in key markets, such as Washington, D.C., Atlanta, Baltimore, and Charlotte, N.C. The multicultural financial centers feature a more open layout than the traditional bank branch, a children's area and weekend hours.

Automated channels

By the end of 1998, 3.4 million U.S. households conducted banking through the Internet. BB&T expanded and enhanced its automated channels during this period. BB&T OnLine, an Internet-based version of its earlier online product, was introduced in October 1999, and a month later Treasury Services unveiled its Internet-based cash management product that provided business clients with an information reporting and transaction system.

In 2000, BB&T had 41,000 online clients and a new department (originally called eBusiness and later renamed the Online and Mobile Channel) was created to oversee the growing delivery channel.

The demand for Internet-based services and the rapid pace of technological change prompted a redesign of the website just a few years later in the spring of 2005. The new layout eliminated redundancies and introduced a consistent design that was easier to navigate.

In March 2008 BB&T launched alerts and mobile banking. These services allowed clients to receive email and text messages for a number of events, including when online statements are available, account balances are low, overdrafts occur and more. Clients could also check balances and transfer funds from their cell phones. Clients quickly saw the value of these services for preventing fraud, identifying mistakes and managing their accounts. In the first three months the Mobile Banking team exceeded their annual enrollment goal for the service.

Monitoring accounts and making transactions got even easier in January 2010 when Mobile Banking released its iPhone application. In the months that followed, BB&T added apps for the Blackberry, iPad and Android devices.

BB&T also made enhancements to its call center and ATM network. As of 2011, the ATM network included more than 2,400 ATMs in 13 states and Washington, D.C. Phone Channel enhancements included detailed self-service options as well as support from client service associates, including those who spoke Spanish.

Student Banking

Recognizing that client loyalty doesn't occur instantly, BB&T began a new student marketing strategy in 2001. The premise of the strategy is that students are the affluent clients of tomorrow.

The heightened focus included enhancements to BB&T's Student Checking account, including lower fees and the convenience of electronic banking. In

2008, BB&T began a "School Spirit" marketing strategy by branding some of its financial centers in close proximity to colleges and universities.

"Choosing the right financial partner is an important decision for students. We feel BB&T can help them with all their financial needs whether an incoming freshman or graduating senior," said Chief Marketing Officer Steve Wiggs. "The branding of these branches with school colors and an account-opening bonus are designed to show our support of the university and encourage students to bank with BB&T."

By 2011, BB&T "School Spirit" financial centers or ATMs were present on the campuses of Clemson University, the University of Georgia, Western Carolina University, East Carolina University, Wofford College, the University of South Carolina, Wake Forest University, UNC-Charlotte, UNC-Wilmington and Carson-Newman College.

BB&T@Work

In 2005, BB&T took its BB&T@Work strategy to a new level by dedicating a sales force to encourage employees of commercial clients to bank with BB&T.

A 2004 pilot program was conducted for the new BB&T@Work program and the results showed great potential. BB&T launched the program with 40 BB&T@Work officers. By 2011, the BB&T@Work sales force had more than doubled. BB&T@Work was the largest single source of new retail transaction accounts opened each month and touted company partners throughout the bank's footprint.

SPORTS MARKETING

As BB&T's acquisition activity declined, advertising budgets previously geared toward introducing BB&T in new markets were channeled into efforts to increase brand awareness.

"NASCAR at the time was, and still is, a very viable sport," Wiggs said. "As a regional bank, we don't have the advertising budgets of our bigger competitors, but we want our sponsorships to reflect the BB&T brand, produce measurable results and make our clients, prospects and employees feel proud of the partnerships. The most recent figure I saw puts the number of NASCAR fans at 75 million. We thought putting our brand on a

Clint Bowyer wins the Crown Royal 400 in Richmond, Va., May 2008. He went on to win the NASCAR Nationwide Series championship in November that same year.

race car would give us exposure not only in the Southeast but nationwide. It was a growth and brand-awareness strategy. We wanted clients and prospects to see that we were a growth company."

In December 2006, BB&T announced it would sponsor a Richard Childress Racing Team in 17 of the season's 35 races. Clint Bowyer was tapped as the driver in the Busch Series (now the Nationwide Series).

Preceding the sponsorship BB&T established the model for measuring client entertainment activities in NASCAR and other professional sports. Client entertainment at the NASCAR races when Bowyer drove the BB&T Chevrolet became a major focus of the program.

The sponsorship gave BB&T an estimated television advertising value of $6.5 million in 2007.

Bowyer drove the No. 2 BB&T Chevy in 25 of the 35 Nationwide Series races in 2008 and cruised into victory lane that November winning the Nationwide Series Championship. He also drove the No. 07 BB&T car in two Sprint Cup Series races, winning in Richmond, Va., in May. The television ad value BB&T realized in 2008 escalated to $32 million due to Bowyer's success.

"It was unheard of for a sponsor to win a Sprint Cup Series race in just its second try," Wiggs said. "It was on the front of the *USA Today* sports page. The article was about the race, but there was the BB&T car – that's the kind of ancillary benefit you get from such sponsorships."

In 2009 Bowyer and the BB&T car (No. 33) graduated to the Sprint Cup Series full-time, participating in 10 races and the All-Star Race. In 2010, Bowyer drove the BB&T car in nine races plus the All-Star event, and in 2011 the BB&T car was on the track for six races plus the All-Star event.

In 2012 as Bowyer and RCR parted ways. BB&T stayed with RCR and became the sponsor of Jeff Burton and the No. 31 Chevrolet.

BB&T has had a number of other, typically regional, sports-related sponsorships and continues to do so. Sponsorships include:

- BB&T Classic basketball invitational in Washington, D.C., since 1999
- BB&T Field at Wake Forest University, Winston-Salem, N.C., since 2007

- BB&T Coastal Field, home of the Myrtle Beach Pelicans minor league baseball team, 2009-2011
- BB&T Ballpark, home of the Winston-Salem Dash minor league baseball team in Winston-Salem, N.C., since 2010
- The Wyndham Championship Presented by BB&T PGA Tour event, since 2008
- A partnership with the Auburn University Athletic Department since 2009
- A partnership with the University of Alabama Athletic Department since 2009
- Official Bank of the Atlantic Coast Conference since 2010
- Miami Heat NBA sponsorship in since 2010
- The Winston Salem-Open professional tennis tournament since 2011

SARBANES-OXLEY ACT

Following a series of corporate accounting scandals, Congress enacted a law in 2002 to protect investors and employees. The act requires top executives of publicly traded companies to personally take responsibility for the accuracy of their company's financial reports. The act was the most sweeping legislation affecting corporate governance, disclosure and financial accountability since the stock market crash of 1929. It requires companies to set up procedures to report significant accounting or auditing problems and protects employees who make such reports.

"BB&T has always been committed to the highest standards of corporate governance," said Scott Reed, chief financial officer at the time. "Unfortunately, some companies did not share those values. Their failures hurt many thousands of shareholders and employees as well as the U.S. economy."

Sarbanes-Oxley represented the beginning of government intervention in day-to-day bank operations and ushered in a time of allocating resources to new regulation. ■

King Takes Helm

On Aug. 27, 2008, BB&T announced John Allison would retire at the end of the year. The Corporate Board voted unanimously to appoint Kelly King as chief executive officer. Allison continued serving as chairman of the board until Dec. 31, 2009, when King assumed that role as well.

THE CLIMATE

It was immediately clear that King was taking the helm at the most challenging time in the country's history since the Great Depression. New Century Financial, a leading subprime mortgage lender, had filed for bankruptcy in April 2007, giving the first signal that something was awry among U.S. mortgage lenders. Shares in other U.S. mortgage banks like Countrywide, which was bought by Bank of America in January 2008, came under pressure.

In March 2008 Bear Stearns announced losses associated with subprime mortgage-backed securities and was soon acquired by JPMorgan Chase. Others would also fail in the coming months. Among them were the prestigious investment banks of Lehman Brothers and Merrill Lynch, both of which reported billion-dollar losses.

Mortgage lenders Fannie Mae and Freddie Mac also revealed substantial losses and were rescued by the government, which feared a run on the dollar by foreign governments who had invested in their bonds, believing the bonds were already guaranteed by the government. The insurance firm AIG, which issued credit guarantees for subprime mortgages, was rescued by the U.S. Treasury.

By the end of 2011, more than 400 financial institutions had been acquired or had gone bankrupt. During the preceding four-year period, the crisis unfolded simultaneously as political leaders talked about tax increases, health care reform and various regulations. Jaw-dropping announcements occurred daily. Stock markets declined, unemployment skyrocketed and the housing market logged considerably higher rates of evictions and foreclosures. The Federal Reserve reported that household wealth had fallen by an estimated $16.4 trillion of net worth between 2007 and early 2009 alone. In the midst of the uncertainty, individuals and businesses alike responded by reducing their outstanding debt, postponing expenditures and being reluctant to invest or borrow.

"It was a little scary," King said. "We were in a position to have a good first-hand sense of what was going on, not just what you see on TV. It was obvious the system was under enormous pressure, and the U.S. was very close to a financial collapse."

King said the events began with the 1999 Financial Services Modernization Act (also called the Gramm-Leach-Bliley Act), which expanded the powers of banks and bank holding companies to sell financial products or services. The act made shopping for financial products more convenient for clients as it cleared the way for banks, securities firms and insurance companies to own each other and cross-sell products and services.

But the act also created opportunities for the "shadow" banking industry – firms such as money market funds, private investment companies and hedge funds that did not have the existing oversight agencies and regulations that banks did. At its peak, 70 percent of all loans had moved out of the traditional banking industry into the shadow banking industry, but by 2011 King said about 50 percent of such loans had returned to the traditional banking system. If the same oversight and regulations had been in place for the shadow banking businesses, some believe that 95 percent of the problems that occurred during the Great Recession could have been prevented.

BB&T's Executive Management met often in the midst of the crisis, including having conference calls on weekends, to discuss the company's risk exposure, the impact on earnings, the latest regulations, reductions in revenue streams and responses needed so employees were prepared to respond to clients about recent events.

"Typically we meet a full day every other week," King said. "During those days, we were meeting several times a day. Everything was so dynamic and volatile, we had to be flexible. Sometimes they were 'we've got to meet right now' meetings."

TROUBLED ASSET RELIEF PROGRAM

In response to the financial crisis, on Oct. 3, 2008, the U.S. government passed the $700 billion Troubled Asset Relief Program (TARP) to provide additional capital to the nation's 19 largest banks and strengthen the financial sector.

"No one really understood the domino effect that Bear Stearns, Lehman Brothers and AIG were going to have on everybody," Chief Financial Officer Daryl Bible said. "TARP was initially supposed to be a way for the government to buy the bad assets, but that really changed."

On Oct. 16, BB&T reported third-quarter net income, totaling $358 million, compared to $444 million in the same quarter of 2007. In the earnings announcement, Allison said that BB&T was not immune to the unprecedented challenges in the financial markets, but it remained a strong and financially sound company with capital levels, debt ratings and earnings among the best in the industry.

On Oct. 27, BB&T announced that it would be among the 19 financial institutions required to participate in the U.S. Treasury Department's Capital Purchase Program to revive the financial sector. It was a move that ran contrary to BB&T's philosophy.

BB&T received $3.1 billion from the government capital infusion plan aimed at restoring liquidity and easing credit in the financial markets. In exchange for the investment, the U.S. Treasury received shares of BB&T preferred stock at a 5-percent annual dividend rate for the first five years. BB&T agreed to repay the government a 9-percent dividend in years six through 10 if shares are not redeemed. The U.S. Treasury also received 10-year warrants to purchase shares of BB&T common stock.

As a result, BB&T's Tier 1 capital ratio, a measure of financial strength and soundness, increased to 12.4 percent from 9.4 percent, significantly higher than the government's safety threshold of 6 percent. BB&T's total capital ratio improved to 17.4 percent from 14.4 percent, notably higher than the minimum government ratio of 10 percent.

"We support the Treasury's efforts to stabilize the credit markets and restore confidence in the financial system," Allison said. "Fortunately, our own strong capital position has allowed us to meet the lending needs of our clients, even during this economic downturn. For us, the additional capital will not only extend and strengthen our lending capacity, but provide other strategic options as well."

The idea to put capital into the banks was a positive step and successfully calmed the marketplace at the time, but the act included language that the government could change the rules in the future.

"By December 2008 it appeared the government would change the rules, and we knew we wanted out of TARP as quickly as possible," Bible said. "Considering the instability in the industry, our ability to be among the first group to exit TARP was a great event."

On May 7, 2009, BB&T announced it had exceeded the government's stress test (officially called the Supervisory Capital Assessment Program) requirements, confirming the company would not be required to raise additional capital. The test also showed that BB&T was one of only nine large financial institutions sufficiently capitalized under a "more adverse" macroeconomic scenario that projected a prolonged and deepening recession.

In the news release King said, "Our capital levels have remained strong throughout this economic downturn, and we continue to lend to creditworthy borrowers in our markets, with loan originations exceeding $6 billion per month. While we do face credit-related challenges, our own adverse-case scenario is more favorable than the government's stress test.

"Now that the stress test is behind us, we will proceed with efforts to implement a capital plan that accomplishes our three strategic objectives," King said. "First, we must remain a very well-capitalized financial institution throughout this credit cycle. We also want to repay the government's investment under the Capital Purchase Program as soon as possible. Finally, our strong capital position will help us take advantage of future opportunities on the other side of this economic correction."

Four days later, BB&T issued a bittersweet release announcing it would repay the TARP funds as well as cut its dividend by 68 percent to 15 cents per share.

BB&T announced it had officially exited TARP on June 17, 2009. BB&T repaid approximately $3.1 billion to the Treasury to repurchase the preferred stock, plus a final dividend payment of about $13.9 million, bringing BB&T's total dividend payments under TARP to approximately $92.7 million.

"This was, in fact, an excellent investment for the American taxpayer," King said.

DIVIDEND

While BB&T would be among the first financial institutions to repay TARP, the company had always taken great pride in its dividend. King said temporarily cutting the dividend was "the worst day in my 37-year career." BB&T's dividend went from 47 cents per share to 15 cents per share, still better than most banks, which cut their dividends to a penny.

BB&T, whose stock was primarily held by individual shareholders, received approximately 300 shareholder letters in response to the dividend cut, according to Alan Greer, director of Investor Relations.

"We read and wrote responses to each letter, and Kelly King read and signed them all," said Greer, who even read about 25 letters while visiting his father at the hospital.

On March 18, 2011, following a second successful stress test, BB&T's board of directors announced a 1-cent increase in the second-quarter dividend and a special 1-cent dividend per common share.

"BB&T is pleased to provide this increase in our dividend and to be in the first group allowed to increase the dividend," King said. "We continue to be one of the strongest capitalized institutions in the industry, and we believe this action confirms that strength.

"We are proud to have maintained the fourth highest dividend yield among S&P 500 banks. We view this as a good first step to further increases in the future," he said.

Inside BB&T, many cheered the dividend increase announcement but none more than the team of nearly 30 employees who worked around the clock preparing for BB&T's stress test submission.

"This team was navigating uncharted waters because there was no precedent for this process," said Chief Financial Officer Daryl Bible. "We are tremendously proud of their efforts and outstanding work."

Dale Davies, Management Reporting manager, said while it seemed like "quite a grind" at times, it was a rewarding endeavor and the team was proud to have been involved in it. "Some employees worked for days straight – barely going home to shower and catch an hour or two of sleep," Davies said. "It was an extraordinary effort, particularly during the holidays."

RISK MANAGEMENT

For financial institutions, including BB&T, credit risk is a critical issue. Going into the recession, BB&T had long enjoyed a superior reputation for its credit risk management practices and its results; however, the extreme stress of the period highlighted the fact that even the best financial institutions had opportunity for improvement. As a growing institution, BB&T needed to thoroughly address not only credit risk, but all risk types, including market, liquidity, reputational, compliance, operational and strategic. In early 2009, the company began forming a comprehensive Risk Management Organization, including a new position, chief risk officer, with Clarke Starnes as the first incumbent.

BB&T began forming a new Risk Management Organization in 2009 to address not only credit risk, but all risk types.

"Every financial institution should decide the amount and types of risk it is willing to accept," Starnes said. "This 'risk appetite' guides the institution in its decision-making. At BB&T, we are in the business of risk management; that is, achieving a balance between risk and return to have satisfactory, predictable outcomes in our businesses. With the risk framework we now have in place, we can identify, assess, measure, control, monitor and report all risk types for BB&T and provide independent oversight for all our risk-taking activities."

In addition to the risk management framework, BB&T made major investments in highly-skilled employees, infrastructure, and technology to build-out the Risk Management Organization. This included the development of a sophisticated economic capital system and related stress-testing regime, a regulatory requirement for all large banking organizations. It also strengthened risk management through numerous policy and process changes including certain reporting relationships. For example, commercial credit officers continued to reside in the communities they served but began reporting to the Risk Management Organization (rather than sales leaders) to improve independence and objectivity.

The extreme stress of the recession also prompted BB&T's leaders to take a critical look at its balance sheet. Prior to the recession, escalating real estate prices created a boom in profitable real estate lending. As a result, BB&T developed a heavy concentration in residential real estate, which presented challenges during the severe economic downturn. In response, BB&T sought to diversify its portfolios to realign the balance sheet. An ongoing portfolio strategy and a limit-setting process were created to avoid future concentrations in real estate or any other asset group.

The extraordinary transformation of BB&T's risk management capabilities from 2009-2011 was necessary to position it as a meaningful participant in the post-recession operating environment.

"While we appreciate who we are and what has made us successful to this point, we have to recognize that BB&T is now a large, complex banking organization and expectations of us are high," Starnes said. "The changes made give us the rigorous risk management and capital planning capabilities we need to identify risk and navigate through challenges to continue helping our clients achieve economic success. With these capabilities in place, our employees, clients, shareholders, and regulators can continue to have the confidence that BB&T is a safe, sound, and very well-run institution."

REGULATORY CHANGES

Numerous regulatory changes were introduced as a result of economic downturn – from more formal, heavily documented lending requirements to new rules that affected banks' fee income. Many of these regulations were created or amended in the Dodd-Frank Wall Street Reform and Consumer Protection Act of 2010.

"The Dodd-Frank Act is approximately 2,300 pages," King said. "No other piece of banking regulation has ever remotely compared. It will create some 350 new rules and regulations for banks. It's been a year since the act was passed and the rules are so complex that regulators have only been able to define about 100 of the new rules for us."

The regulations took a toll on BB&T's revenue, said Donna Goodrich, Deposit Services manager.

"To date, we've calculated a $385 million impact to BB&T's revenue stream," she said. "To satisfy our shareholders, we're looking for ways that we can make up that lost revenue, and we've identified how we can reclaim about half of it. But it will take time to roll out new products and services to accomplish it."

A few of the new regulations created during this time included:

Fees related to credit and debit cards were among those affected by new regulations.

CARD Act – The Credit Card Accountability Responsibility and Disclosure (CARD) Act of 2009 went into full effect in February 2010 and dramatically altered credit card lending.

The most notable changes were eliminating or reducing fees. BB&T already had many consumer-friendly practices so the CARD Act did not dramatically change the way it operated its credit card business.

Reg. E – Regulation E, effective August 2010, required all banks to obtain client consent for authorizing or paying debit card or ATM transactions that overdrew their accounts. Massive amounts of client communications were distributed explaining the pros and cons of both decisions – to opt-in or opt-out of BB&T paying transactions creating overdrafts.

The Volcker Rule – This rule restricted the amount of capital banks could invest in private equity and hedge funds.

The Durbin Amendment – The Durbin Amendment, which applies to banks with more than $10 billion in assets, gave the Federal Reserve the power to regulate the amount of debit card interchange fees banks collect from merchants. Merchants pay these fees to cover the bank's cost of processing the transaction and assuming the fraud risk associated with debit card transactions. The cap was expected to reduce industry-wide bank fees by approximately $9.4 billion annually and sent banks searching for new ways to make up the lost revenue.

The Consumer Financial Protection Bureau (CFPB) – The new regulatory body was given independent authority to set rules for the banking industry, examine banks to see if they are compliant, and execute enforcement actions. This new bureau created great concern in the industry since it operated independently of the Federal Reserve, FDIC or Office of the Comptroller of the Currency, and was not required to emphasize financial safety and soundness in conjunction with consumer protection.

"It's too soon to tell, but the CFPB has the potential to drive the banking system's profitability and capital down so low that the whole system gets more risky," King said.

With all the new regulations, industry insiders began to anticipate further consolidation.

"With the rising costs associated with all the regulations, there ultimately has to be more consolidation in order to spread the rising fixed costs over more variable dollars," Chris Henson said. "Frankly, a lot of the systems we're implementing can work for a $500 billion bank as well as they can for a $150 billion bank."

Bible agreed with Henson, but added that BB&T could not rely solely on acquisitions for future growth.

"There is still a lot of consolidation to occur, but it's important to stay focused on organic growth because you can't count on winning the acquisition bids," Bible said in 2011. "It's a very competitive environment. BB&T's emphasis on organic growth is something we do well, but it is increasingly challenging. We expect a slow growth environment for the next few years, so we'll continue to work to ensure our costs don't grow faster than our revenue. We have to have positive operating leverage to have a strong company."

COLONIAL BANK ACQUISITION

Aug. 14, 2009, was an exciting and historic day for BB&T. The company publicly announced it had acquired the banking operations of Colonial Bank of Montgomery, Ala. This was possible in part because of BB&T's strong capital position.

Colonial, which was founded in 1981, had more than 4,500 employees and was one of the 30 largest financial holding companies in the nation, making it BB&T's largest merger to date.

The acquisition of Colonial's $20 billion in deposits and $22 billion in assets made BB&T the eighth largest bank in the nation based on assets. *Time* magazine even named the deal No. 3 in its list of Top 10 Best Business Deals for 2009.

In the FDIC-assisted deal, BB&T assumed very little of the failed institution's risk. BB&T reopened Colonial's 354 banking offices as branches of BB&T and Colonial depositors continued to be insured by the FDIC.

The acquisition gave BB&T the No. 4 market share in Alabama and No. 5 in Florida, two key markets in the Southeast. Colonial also gave BB&T its first banking presence in Texas.

"The Colonial acquisition was possibly the most outstanding merger and acquisition BB&T has ever done," said President of Community Banking Ricky Brown. "We obviously learned about Colonial's position through the FDIC. We didn't have much time to prepare, but our Finance and Legal teams did an outstanding job on the bid. We made an aggressive bid and won by just a little. That's what you want – not to leave much on the table."

Colonial Bank represented the largest merger in BB&T's history.

The acquisition team knew if BB&T won, the company had to be in a position to move forward quickly. The bidding process began on a Monday, and the BB&T acquisition team knew if it won they wanted BB&T branch "buddies" in every Colonial office by that Friday.

BB&T received word that it had won the bid after normal business hours that Thursday. In true BB&T fashion, more than 425 employees were deployed to Colonial's markets to work side-by-side as buddies with Colonial employees and their clients.

"You had to work as if you were going to get the bid," Henson said. "It happened fast – like a shotgun wedding. We were fortunate that the Colonial employees were ready to move forward, which helped us start the process beginning day one. We were able to quickly affect changes that would normally take six to nine months."

Long-time employees and clients alike were amazed by the timeline and the success.

"I have never seen another merger quite like this," said Wilson, N.C.-based Danny Daniels, a veteran of nearly 40 years with BB&T and president the Eastern Region at the time. Daniels selected 16 people who flew to Colonial destinations in Mobile and nearby Baldwin County, Ala.

"We couldn't tell them where they would go because we didn't know," Daniels said. "We told them, 'We just need you to be prepared to work in another location for seven days.'"

Daniels said his team members, who were not among those able to drive to their locations, got the go-ahead while waiting in a charter airplane facility. It was 6:08 p.m. on Thursday, Aug. 13. They arrived at their South Alabama destinations around 8:30 p.m. Because of the secrecy of the FDIC deal, they couldn't tell their families where they were until they entered their assigned Colonial branches at 5:30 p.m. on Friday, Aug. 14.

In Madison, Ala., BB&T's Mike Sox was busy telling his bank's story as he greeted a client at the Madison Boulevard branch near Huntsville, Ala.

"I assured him that he was with one of the strongest financial institutions in the country," Sox said. "I told him we were glad to have him and wanted to keep his business."

A senior analyst with a weapons system contracting firm, the client had served in elevated command positions with the U.S. Army in Korea and Vietnam as well as with NATO in Germany. He was so impressed with BB&T that he sent Sox his impressions in a letter.

"The speed with which BB&T acted to get representatives to the locations of its most recent acquisition is nothing short of mind-boggling," the client wrote, noting that it was a logistical maneuver that he wasn't sure the U.S. armed forces could duplicate. "BB&T is to be highly commended for taking immediate and decisive actions to allay any fears by the employees as well as the customers."

To prevent the Colonial deal from diluting shareholder interest, on Aug. 18, 2009, BB&T announced a common stock offering of 33.45 million shares at $26 per share. The net proceeds were used as tangible common equity and Tier 1 regulatory capital.

"We'd never raised capital for an acquisition in our history," Bible said. "Most banks never have. We didn't have established relationships with a lot of institutional investors. To be able to do that is a real credit to Kelly and how he runs the Executive Management team."

Chris Henson, chief operating officer, said prior to our initial common stock offering to repay TARP, BB&T retail (individual) investors owned approximately 70 percent of BB&T's stock. Following our subsequent stock offering to finance the acquisition of Colonial, institutional investors owned approximately 50 percent.

The FDIC thought BB&T was "very effective," Bible added. "They thought we did an awesome job of handling the transaction, calming the market and stopping the run on Colonial Bank that was occurring."

REFLECTING AND LOOKING FORWARD

As 2011 came to a close, BB&T's Executive Management team reflected on the past several years and began looking forward to the company's 140th birthday in 2012.

Considering the day-to-day challenges, BB&T fared extremely well during the recession. The Executive Management team attributed this to several factors – from not engaging in risky mortgage lending practices to having other lines of business, such as BB&T Insurance, Corporate Banking, Lending and Wealth Management, that made strong contributions to earnings when the retail banking business was tight.

"Lending and Insurance Services really contributed significantly to our earnings," Henson said. "So the diversification in our revenue base performed exactly as it should have during a down market."

Reflecting on the challenges of recent years, Henson said he would do it all again.

"If you'd told me in 2007 that we were getting ready to go through the Great Recession, the worst downturn since the Great Depression; that we were going to see Bear Stearns, Wachovia, Washington Mutual and Lehman Brothers fail and Merrill Lynch be bought by Bank of America; and BB&T was going to make money every quarter, our brand was going to improve and we were going to have the fastest revenue growth of anyone in our peer group, I would have signed up for that immediately. But, it's not surprising since we're a value-based organization," he said.

Leon Wilson and Donna Goodrich characterized these past several years as the biggest challenges of their careers, but they are pleased with the results.

"This last year (2011) has been a year of revolutionary change as we've gotten out a blank sheet of paper and tried to figure out how to replace lost revenues in the midst of addressing so many regulatory changes," Goodrich said. "It's also been disheartening how bankers have been negatively portrayed when we know BB&T didn't participate in risky practices and truly strives to help the communities we serve."

"There were no rules or precedents," Wilson said. "And, it wasn't as if you had one or two new challenges to work on. There were more and new challenges on a daily, sometimes hourly, basis. You didn't want to open the Wall Street Journal, because you didn't know what other disaster was going to be in the headlines. It was a very negative time.

"It would be a sheer luxury to come to work and do your normal job," Wilson said. "I don't remember what it was like not to be fighting off the next attack, dealing with the next crisis or figuring out what this legislation or that regulation means. But if you look back at BB&T's financial performance over the last few years, we're still making money. Most banks can't say that."

Starnes echoed Wilson's sentiments.

"At times it felt daunting," Starnes said. "We had daily discussions to make sure we understood our risk and could fund the bank properly. We talked about what we would do if we experienced the deposit runs that occurred at other organizations. It was almost a surreal experience.

"I couldn't be more proud of being part of the team that led this effort for BB&T. Every member of Executive Management took their level of responsibility in this process very seriously. We were highly focused on making sure this company survived and had an opportunity to grow stronger as we come out of this crisis. We were very concerned about our clients, communities, employees and shareholders. I think what we've been able to accomplish is pretty good validation that we were successful."

And although the banking industry has a tarnished reputation to overcome, Steve Wiggs and Ricky Brown said BB&T employees can take pride in the company's accomplishments and know it is well positioned for the future.

"Our industry has a big black eye that has been cast upon us for things BB&T didn't really take part in," Wiggs said. "It was a time when everybody was bashing bankers, which was unfortunate. A bank is just a reflection of the economy, and we do a lot of good things in our communities beyond lending money to companies so they can create employment. So our industry is trying to work our way out of that now. It was a crisis we could have never envisioned, and we have a tremendous sense of achievement for having navigated through it phenomenally well."

Brown said BB&T should be proud of its historical accomplishments.

"We've come through every crisis – the Great Depression, World War II, the '60s and social unrest, the savings and loan debacle of the '80s and the recent financial crisis," Brown said. "We've come through them and we're positioned well for the future. Employees can take pride in the role they have played in BB&T's longevity, our resilience and creativity." ∎

Unwavering Commitment

What makes BB&T different from other financial institutions? How has BB&T avoided so many of the scandals that have affected other companies?

It's the company's long-standing, unwavering commitment to its vision, mission and values. These tenets drive a rich culture that permeates the organization and guide everything from evaluating acquisition prospects, to charitable contributions and day-to-day decision making.

BB&T's retired executives say the company had a commitment to these beliefs well before they were even committed to paper.

"We always talked about our continuity of purpose and making sure our decisions were consistent with our vision, mission and values," Ken Chalk said.

Scott Reed agreed, adding that Executive Management always emphasized doing things with great integrity.

"That was true even if it cost us money," Reed said. "I remember several situations where we could have done things differently and saved money or made more money, but we didn't. We stuck on the right path and did the right things with high integrity and honesty. If BB&T ever gives up its integrity and its approach to dealing with vendors and shareholders and certainly customers and fellow employees, it will be lost and not prosper the way it has."

During the challenges of the recent Great Recession, Ricky Brown said everyone at BB&T was guided by BB&T's vision, mission and values, especially the Community Bank employees who most often interact with clients.

"Our front-line employees were dealing with clients who were losing their jobs and their homes, and having trouble paying their bills. Some of our employees' own families were facing some of these struggles," Brown said.

"We were dealing with it all day at work and at home in the evenings. But, our employees worked diligently to meet our clients' needs as never before. Kelly once said 'relationships are born in adversity,' and in these challenging times we turned to our culture – vision, mission and values – as an anchor. We didn't have to search for direction, it was right there to guide us, to help us nurture and strengthen our relationships. It was definitely a differentiator. It's an extraordinary culture."

And Daryl Bible said BB&T was able to weather the Great Recession because of its strength in ethical credit underwriting and its ability to change while maintaining the foundation of its vision, mission and values.

Time and time again, BB&T has found this to be true.

"The more the world and the financial services industry change, the more we need the anchor of our values," John Allison said.

EMINENT DOMAIN

BB&T's 2006 position on a Supreme Court decision that cleared the way for the use of eminent domain to seize private property for shopping malls, condominiums and other private development projects is another example of how the company has been guided by its vision, mission and values.

On Jan. 25, 2006, BB&T issued a news release about BB&T's position on eminent domain. The release stated that BB&T would make no loans to developers who planned to build commercial projects on land taken from private citizens through the power of eminent domain. While BB&T's Executive Management team considered the possibility that it could lose some commercial clients, the corporate board unanimously supported their decision.

The eminent domain announcement was lauded by the media, clients, employees and shareholders. It led to national TV interviews with John Allison and a nationally syndicated radio interview with Chief Credit Officer Ken Chalk. Media coverage included articles in *The Wall Street Journal, USA Today, The New York Times* and *Toronto Free Press.*

One editorial after another declared BB&T an anomaly, a large corporation willing to put values before profits. The announcement resulted in nearly 1,000 positive emails, nearly 100 letters and an unknown number of phone calls.

"I guess it shouldn't surprise me how cynical people are about businesses," Allison said. "They think we'd do anything for a buck. With eminent domain we heard time and time again how surprised people were to see a company actually take a stand on principle. CEOs from other large banks called me to congratulate me. When I asked if they were also going to oppose eminent domain they said they didn't take positions on public policy. Not a single bank joined BB&T in this position."

THE LIGHTHOUSE PROJECT

While BB&T has always supported the communities it serves through corporate and regional charitable contributions, The Lighthouse Project directly addressed the needs of the communities BB&T serves as never before. In 2009, King recognized the need for more hands-on community involvement and launched The Lighthouse Project.

This effort gave BB&T employees paid time off to help the many overwhelmed and underfunded local nonprofit organizations through volunteer service and corporate financial local support. It was a way to shine a beacon of light into a world that for some seemed somewhat dark and hopeless.

On regional visits King heard employee after employee share emotional stories about a brother or sister who had lost a job or clients in financial distress. He decided to create a way that BB&T could help employees alleviate some of the suffering in their communities.

"I could see the pain in our employees' eyes," he said. "Their community and their families were really suffering. So we conceptualized The Lighthouse Project. I was very excited and pleased by how our organization embraced it immediately. It's probably what I'm most proud of in my career in terms of really a visible, tangible way we live out our mission."

Donna Goodrich said The Lighthouse Project was the right thing to focus on at the right time.

"Kelly's heart was focused on helping others in these difficult times," Goodrich said. "It reaffirmed our belief in our mission. Our vision, mission and values are ingrained in everything we do. People at BB&T care deeply about others, we invest in people."

Bryan Larsen's "Heritage and Hope" illustration used on the cover of the 2011 Annual Report depicts BB&T as an anchor of strength and stability for 140 years.

Since the inception of The Lighthouse Project, BB&T employees have led more than 3,200 community-service projects, volunteered more than 150,000 hours, and improved the quality of life for more than 5 million people. In 2011, 85 percent of BB&T employees participated, with most finding the experience so personally rewarding that they voted to continue the effort in 2012.

THE PERFECT CLIENT EXPERIENCE

In 2002 BB&T branded its internal service culture the Perfect Client Experience (PCE). It is a unique process created to ensure the desired day-to-day client service behaviors are actionable and measurable. The ultimate goal is to ensure clients have a consistent experience regardless of whether they interact with BB&T at a branch, through online or mobile banking, Phone24 or an ATM.

"We are living and breathing our mission through the Perfect Client Experience," King said. "It gives us renewed focus on providing the best service to our clients each and every day."

BB&T's Perfect Client Experience gold seal, which includes the client service behaviors, is trademarked.

The PCE behaviors, based on client feedback, provide reliable, responsive, empathetic and competent service in everything the company does. Beyond these are four steps employees strive to perform consistently – welcome clients, help clients, thank clients and assist clients who may be experiencing problems. They serve as the foundation for BB&T's business model.

The service culture also has operational components – training, measurement, coaching and rewards. A PCE Council, which consists primarily of Executive Management team members, evaluates the service measurements and identifies refinements quarterly.

"PCE and BB&T's Vision, Mission and Values have a direct link," Chris Henson said. "At BB&T you can't separate sales from service. It's about doing the right thing. When employees are happy and engaged, they do the right things for clients, who benefit and enjoy the whole relationship better.

By providing the Perfect Client Experience, you earn the money necessary to support your communities at the level you want and return a portion of the profit to the shareholders for their investment."

Several core beliefs that reflect the essence of PCE include:

- I make a difference in the lives of my clients. Banking is a noble profession.

- I will deliver the level of service I expect from others.

- I want to deepen my understanding of my clients and their needs with each contact.

- I have a responsibility to know as much as possible about my clients and BB&T's products. This knowledge empowers me to offer the right products and services to my clients.

"The Perfect Client Experience is the service we provide," Brown said. "Integrated Relationship Management is the way we refer business from one area of the organization to another to help our clients meet their financial goals. IRM and PCE bring our mission to life and help us achieve our vision. It's all consistent with our values. We don't focus on selling clients the products we want them to have. We provide clients with the products and services they need to achieve their goals."

BB&T's commitment to the Perfect Client Experience will remain fundamental to our culture.

THE BB&T BRAND

Chief Marketing Officer Steve Wiggs said BB&T's culture, vision, mission and values are the essence of its brand.

"We have a brand and a company that has been around for 140 years. While BB&T adapts to change, we've learned how important our history of safety and soundness is," Wiggs said. "It helps us reassure clients, and it's critical that we protect BB&T's brand and reputation. Whether it's what we're doing today relative to 140 years ago or what we do today that's relative 140 years from now, what comes to mind is BB&T cares about its employees and clients. It always comes back to making the right decisions. When people join BB&T from other banks they say, 'You don't know what it's like outside of BB&T.' So they come to appreciate what a really special company it is."

Sharing Knowledge for a
Brighter Direction   **BB&T**

Sharing Knowledge with North Carolina Clients and Communities For 140 Years.

The facade above is on BB&T's oldest remaining building, built in Wilson, North Carolina in 1903. For over 140 years, BB&T has been guided by strong values – including always doing what's in the best interest of our clients and sharing sound financial knowledge so our clients can make more informed decisions. Values that, like this 109-year-old building, have stood the test of time. Talk to us today about your banking needs and know how it feels to know more.

BANKING · INSURANCE · INVESTMENTS · BBT.COM

BB&T celebrated its 140-year birthday in 2012. The milestone was recognized in advertising and with internal events held periodically throughout the year.

BB&T University helps support the company's mission of creating a place where employees can learn, grow and be fulfilled in their work.

BB&T UNIVERSITY

Part of BB&T's mission charges the company with "creating a place where employees can learn, grow and be fulfilled in their work." BB&T University serves as a major source of learning and growth for employees. BB&T considers the human mind to be the primary natural resource capable of providing a competitive advantage.

"BB&T University helps us create effective leaders," Allison said. "Effective leaders develop strategies to turn their vision into reality."

A TRIBUTE TO LEADERSHIP

The foresight and courage of BB&T's late Chief Executive Officers Thorne Gregory and Vincent Lowe to hire and empower a group of five young professionals set the stage for BB&T's success.

During a five-year period in the early 1970s, Gregory and Lowe hired John Allison, Kelly King, Henry Williamson, Ken Chalk and Scott Reed – all of whom were recent graduates with MBAs. They joined BB&T based on a desire to revolutionize the company and expand the bank beyond Eastern North Carolina. The new leaders were enthusiastic about the company's potential and the roles they could play in its success.

"We were very fortunate to have Thorne Gregory and Vincent Lowe as CEOs prior to John Allison," King said. "They deserve a lot of credit for hiring us and supporting our vision for what BB&T could become. They recognized BB&T needed young talent to challenge the existing organization."

With Gregory's support, the newcomers worked closely with Lowe, who had a reputation for being a bit gruff and intimidating. However, Lowe took the group under his wing and helped each of them develop in their various roles.

"Thorne made a lot of very good decisions for the bank," Reed said. "He was an excellent man, who befriended all of us. Vincent acted tough sometimes, but it was a façade. Down deep, he was a really nice guy."

Tension soon developed between some of the older BB&T managers and the newcomers. The older managers often took issue with the changes and growth strategies the newcomers proposed.

The five executives who set BB&T's direction for more than 25 years are (from left)
Ken Chalk, Henry Williamson, Scott Reed, Kelly King and John Allison.

Photo courtesy of *Triad Business Journal*

"One day Thorne asked me how things were going," King said. "He was a little surprised when I told him things were not going well with the younger managers and if things didn't change they might not stay at BB&T."

King suggested Gregory meet with the five MBAs, whose paths crossed often enough during business hours that they had become friends outside of the office as well. Gregory agreed. He and Lowe met with them and listened to their concerns.

"The bank was staid, very conservative, not very aggressive," Reed said. "We didn't have a focused strategy on what the company should become. We told Thorne and Vincent we either wanted to pursue other opportunities or we wanted to see some pretty drastic changes at BB&T. And, we wanted to have some input into those changes. I think Thorne and Vincent did a lot of talking and soul-searching about whether to stay with the opinion of the older management or move in our direction."

Gregory listened. He gave Lowe responsibility for the bank's operations, and Lowe made the group of five younger men members of the Executive Management team.

"It took a tremendous amount of courage on Thorne's part to ultimately make some of the changes that had to be made, and he did it with class," Williamson said. "It was one of those pivotal events that make a good company a great one. It was the springboard that changed the history of BB&T forever."

Unfortunately, Gregory died in the midst of the transition. Lowe succeeded Gregory as CEO, but only held the position for seven years before he also passed away unexpectedly. The board appointed Allison as CEO in 1989.

"Naming one of us as the new CEO wasn't an obvious choice for the board," Allison said. "They certainly could have decided to hire someone more mature, with more experience. We weren't kids, but there was nobody as young as we were running a bank. It was both exhilarating and scary."

The new Executive Management Team was concerned about being bought, and this was an opportunity for BB&T to become more aggressive. But, the economy collapsed in the later part of '89, so they began their expanded roles in the face of a major economic correction.

"When Vincent passed away, we really had to rely on each other," King said. "At that time, it was unusual to have five MBAs, about the same age, who were all hired within a few short years. It's even more unusual that we all stayed together. I think we did that because we enjoyed working together. We had a common purpose. We had a vision for BB&T, and we complemented each other."

An article in *The Business Journal* serving the Triad-area of North Carolina called Allison "a philosopher" with low-profile strength. King, then president, was the senior sales leader known for rallying the troops. Williamson, the chief operating officer, was the deep thinker who counter balanced Allison and King's progressive approach. Reed, then chief financial officer, was known for considering how their decisions affected others, particularly BB&T employees. And Chalk, then chief credit officer, consistently watched the details and identified facts the others might have missed.

"We developed a strong consensus building bond," King said. "We were fortunate that each of us brought a different set of strengths to the table. Like a football or basketball team, we learned to play our roles well for the purpose of the team. While we disagreed at times, we never questioned each other's integrity. I think that was a very important reason why we stayed together throughout our careers.

"When people say who should get the most credit for BB&T today, I say Vincent Lowe. He was the one who brought in the leadership group that built and guided BB&T for more than 25 years. Thorne gets a tremendous amount of credit for supporting Vincent and our team as we took BB&T from a small Eastern North Carolina bank to one of the largest, safest and most secure financial institutions in the country."

The BB&T we know today stems from the foundation Gregory and Lowe laid for this team of young business leaders. From that, they emphasized and built upon BB&T's vision, mission and values, which paved the way for the company's enduring and respected culture.

ANCHORED IN CULTURE, POSITIONED FOR SUCCESS

BB&T celebrated its 140th anniversary in 2012. The organization participated in a yearlong celebration, which included a variety of anniversary-related activities. Chairman and CEO Kelly King reaffirmed BB&T's unwavering commitment to its vision, mission and values, and staying anchored in its culture.

King refers to BB&T's vision, mission and values as "non-negotiables." They are recognized as the company's hallmark.

After King became chairman and CEO he organized the BB&T values John Allison had previously committed to paper to further show how they drive success. BB&T focuses on values in terms of character, judgment, success and happiness.

"Being honest and having integrity is the foundation of good character," he said. "It's the bedrock of our values. You have integrity if you live honestly and adhere to your values consistently. Judgment is about making sound decisions based on reality, reason and independent thinking. In this highly politicized and emotional environment, exercising good judgment is critical.

Chairman and CEO Kelly King developed a model to illustrate how BB&T's values drive success.

And success is about being productive, working well as a team and maintaining a sense of justice. At BB&T we strive to maintain a workplace where employees can draw a sense of self-esteem and pride in their work."

Throughout a person's career at BB&T, we want them to have a strong sense of self-esteem from doing what's right and making the lives of others better, King added.

"We continue to reinforce and live by our values today – just like we did when I began my career," he said. "BB&T was founded in a rural setting, serving agricultural clients. Our culture stems from those early days and that environment of wholesome values. I think it formed the essence of our culture that has continued to this day."

BB&T has come a long way since its modest beginning in 1872. The small community bank Alpheus Branch and Thomas Jefferson Hadley began has grown into a multi-dimensional financial services organization.

North Carolina's oldest bank entered the 21st century as one of the safest and soundest financial institutions in the country. While the company will continue to grow and evolve, King maintains that its success depends on preserving the vision, mission, values and culture that have served the company well and are uniquely BB&T.

"Our culture is driven by these tenets," King said. "Being anchored in our culture has helped us avoid the scandals that have plagued other companies in recent years. Our values and culture guide us as we help our clients achieve success and will serve as the catalysts for future growth in a rapidly changing and unpredictable world."

As we reflect with great pride on our heritage, all of us at BB&T anticipate tomorrow's challenges with tremendous enthusiasm. The men and women who will lead this organization into the future know they must remember the lessons of the past as they fulfill BB&T's mission of serving its clients, communities, associates and shareholders.

These leaders will continue to add to the BB&T legacy – a tradition with a future. ∎

Biographies of Chairmen and Chief Executive Officers of BB&T

TABLE VI

Chairmen of the Board

Branch Banking and Trust Company

Selby Hurt Anderson	August 1, 1915 – January 23, 1962
Honorary Chairman	January 23, 1962 – March 1, 1962
Frederick Louis Carr	January 23, 1962 – August 21, 1979
Honorary Chairman	August 21, 1979 – July 19 1981
Garland S. Tucker, Jr.	August 21, 1979 – March 17, 1987
L. Vincent Lowe, Jr.	March 17, 1987 – July 7, 1989
John A. Allison IV	July 11, 1989 – December 31, 2009
Kelly. S. King	January 1, 2010 – present

BB&T Financial Corporation*

Thorne Gregory	July 1, 1974 – February 18, 1982
L. Vincent Lowe, Jr.	February 16, 1982 – July 7, 1989
John A. Allison IV	July 11, 1989 – December 31, 2009
Kelly S. King	January 1, 2010—present

Chief Executive Officers

Branch Banking and Trust Company

Alpheus Branch	1872 – January 3, 1893
William Preston Simpson	January 3, 1893 – June 3, 1896
Henry Groves Connor	June 22, 1896 – January 8, 1907
Jacob Cecil Hales	January 8, 1907 – January 5, 1913
Selby Hurt Anderson	January 18, 1913 – August 1, 1915
Sidney Graham Mewborn	August 1, 1915 – October 3, 1924
Herbert Dalton Bateman	October 3, 1924 – December 31, 1952
Joshua Ernest Paschall	January 1, 1953 – December 31, 1963
John Lafayette Satchwell	January 1, 1964 – December 31, 1972
Thorne Gregory	January 1, 1973 – February 13, 1982
L. Vincent Lowe, Jr.	February 16, 1982 – July 7, 1989
John A. Allison IV	July 11, 1989 – December 31, 2008
Kelly S. King	January 1, 2009—present

BB&T Financial Corporation*

Thorne Gregory	July 1, 1974 – February 13, 1982
L. Vincent Lowe, Jr.	February 16, 1982 – July 7, 1989
John A. Allison IV	July 11, 1989 – December 31, 2008
Kelly S. King	January 1, 2009—present

* Branch Corporation was changed to BB&T Financial Corporation in 1988. The name was changed again to Southern National Corporation when the bank merged with Southern National Corporation on February 28, 1995. Southern National was renamed BB&T Corporation on May 16, 1997.

ALPHEUS BRANCH[1]

Alpheus Branch was born near Tillery on May 7, 1843, the son of Captain Samuel Warren and Mary Branch. He spent his childhood in Halifax County, where his father was an extensive planter. Alpheus attended Deems Military Academy in Wilson, Horner School in Oxford, and Trinity College, which he left to join the Confederate Army as a member of the Scotland Neck Cavalry. His military record reveals that he served with honor. He became interested in military organizations, and after the war served as an honorary member of the Wilson Light Infantry Company.

After his discharge from the army, he returned to his native Halifax County and became successful enough as a farmer to act as private banker for his neighbors.

On November 7, 1865, he married Nannie Barnes, only daughter of General Joshua Barnes, one of Wilson's founders. By 1869 they had moved to Wilson and the mercantile firm, Branch and Company, was established. In 1872 Mr. Branch and Thomas Jefferson Hadley established the firm Branch and Hadley, the forerunner of Branch Banking and Trust Company. In 1887 he bought Mr. Hadley's interest and changed the name to Branch and Company, Bankers.

Mr. and Mrs. Branch were the parents of six children. They built and occupied a house at the corner of Nash and Pine streets, which later was known as the Clark house. Then they built another house at the corner of Nash Street and Park Avenue. It was here that Mr. Branch died on January 3, 1893.

Mr. Branch did much to further the interests of Wilson's public school system and was also instrumental in promoting the Wilson tobacco market. The January 10, 1893, issue of the *Wilson Mirror* proclaimed him the "… wealthiest, most influential and most useful citizen … broad-gauged and liberal minded … he was the most affable and delightful gentleman we ever met, and no one could surpass him in those courtly graces and princely courtesies which always distinguish and proclaim the cultured and polished well bred gentleman … "

WILLIAM PRESTON SIMPSON[2]

William Preston Simpson was born in Halifax County near Enfield on September 30, 1851. He was appointed by Alpheus Branch as co-executor of Mr. Branch's will, and he took over the management of the bank when Mr. Branch died in 1893. He remained president until his death on June 3, 1896.

Mr. Simpson was a highly intelligent and very dignified man, and his sudden death was a shock to the community. On June 5 the *Raleigh News and Observer* stated: "Mr. Simpson was a most admirable business man, and a most excellent citizen, and dying at the high noon of brilliant usefulness and prosperity, his untimely death will be most sadly deplored, for it makes a void that no one else can fill."

HENRY GROVES CONNOR[3]

Henry Groves Connor was born in Wilmington on July 3, 1852, son of David and Mary Groves Connor. He grew up and received his early education in Wilson, where he began his practice of law in 1873. In 1885 he was elected a member of the State Senate, and that year he was also appointed judge of the Superior Court. He resigned in 1893 to re-enter private practice. On the death of W. P. Simpson in 1896 he became president of Branch and Company, Bankers. He was a member of the Lower House of the Legislature from 1899 until 1901 and was its speaker in 1899. In 1900 Branch and Company, Bankers, became Branch Banking Company with Mr. Connor as president. He served in that capacity until 1907, when he resigned to devote his time to his duties as an associate justice of the Supreme Court of North Carolina, to which he had been appointed in 1902. In 1909 he was appointed judge of the United States District Court for the Eastern District. Mr. Connor remained on the Federal bench until his death on November 23, 1924.

Judge Connor was a Democrat, a member of the Episcopal Church and received an honorary doctor of laws degree from the University of North Carolina in 1908. He and his wife, Kate Whitfield, became the parents of twelve children. Their oldest son, George W., was for a time associated with Branch Banking Company and then became judge of the North Carolina Supreme Court. The second son, Henry Groves Connor II, was a State Senator and member of the House of Representatives. Another son, R. D. W. Connor, was Kenan Professor of History and Government at the University of North Carolina and was the first United States Archivist.

Judge Connor's daughter, Mrs. Margaret Connor Simpson, remembers that her father was calm even in the face of emergency. When she was a young girl, they lost their house as the result of a fire. Her father's overseer rushed to the court where the Judge was presiding and shouted the news as he ran up to the Judge. Judge Connor asked him to be seated, dismissed the court and only then went to see about his burning house.

JACOB CECIL HALES[4]

Jacob Cecil Hales was born on March 21, 1864, son of John J. and Delaney Daniel Hales. One of Wilson's outstanding scholars, he attended the Wilson Collegiate Institute, where he pursued eleven studies (about twice the usual number), and graduated with an average grade of 95. *The Wilson Advance* described him as being "blessed by the Creator with a finer mind than any other student that we have ever had." He became associated with Branch and Company, Bankers, in 1889 and was elected president in 1907. Along with other prominent bankers of the time, he attended the organizational meeting of the North Carolina Bankers Association held at Morehead City on July 24, 1897.

Mr. Hales was successful in many enterprises besides banking. He had an interest in the Fidelity Building (later known as the Gold Professional Building), the New Briggs Hotel, a lumber business, a milling business, the Wilson Light and Power Company and was one of the original charter members and on the Board of Directors of Jefferson Standard Life Insurance Company. He served as Master of his Masonic Lodge and as substitute mayor for a brief time.

He was married in 1887, and he and his wife became the parents of six children. One of his sons, Felix S. Hales, writes about his father: "He loved his family, was patient with his children, although stern. He helped them with their school work and devoted much time with them in play... In my mind, he believed in the highest of ideals and I remember him with love and respect, even though he did give me the whip occasionally." Another son, C. S. Hales, says, "He was also a very good chess player and taught me how to play the game, but I could never beat him."

Mr. Hales was a deeply religious man and wrote a book entitled *That They All May Be One* in which he advocated a union of all Protestant churches. He died on January 5, 1913, and in tribute to him many of the business firms of Wilson closed their doors during the funeral.

SELBY HURT ANDERSON[5]

Selby Hurt Anderson was associated with Branch Banking and Trust Company for 58 years. He became a member of the Board of Directors in 1904, and served as president from 1913 until 1915, when he was elected chairman of the board. In 1962 he was elected honorary chairman.

Mr. Anderson was born in Halifax County, Virginia, on February 4, 1874, son of Thomas McKencie and Rebecca Milner Anderson. When he was a young man in his twenties, he moved to Wilson with his parents. He and his father were among the pioneers in the tobacco industry in Wilson, and with his brother, Will P., he founded the Watson Warehouse. He was also in the leaf division of the business, establishing with H. G. Whitehead the firm Whitehead and Anderson Company. He was one of the original stockholders and a director of Jefferson Standard Life Insurance Company.

On August 7, 1901, Mr. Anderson married Ellen Branch, daughter of Alpheus Branch, and they were the parents of one daughter, Marie Rebecca (Mrs. Rom P. Watson, Jr.). Mr. Anderson was a member of the Episcopal Church and served as vestryman. He was awarded the 50 Year Club membership certificate by the North Carolina Bankers Association in 1961. Mr. Anderson died on March 1, 1962.

SIDNEY GRAHAM MEWBORN[6]

Sidney Graham Mewborn was born on November 8, 1868, in Greene County, son of Levi Jesse Hardy and Ruth Whitted Mewborn. He was reared in that county and received his early education there. He studied law at the University of North Carolina and began his private practice in Wilson. In 1895 he was elected a member of the State Legislature from Greene County. Before becoming president of Branch Banking and Trust Company in 1915, he served as clerk of the Wilson County Superior Court. In 1924 he resigned his presidency to become judge of the Wilson County General Court. He remained a director of the bank until his death on July 9, 1937.

Judge Mewborn was an active member of the First Christian Church. He was a member of all the local York Rite Bodies of Masonry and Sudan Shrine Temple. He was Past Master of the local Masonic Lodge, Past High Priest of Mount Lebanon Chapter, Royal Arch, Masons, Past Master Mount Lebanon Council and Past Commander of the Mount Lebanon Commandery. He was secretary of all the local Masonic organizations, a position he held for almost 15 years.

Judge Mewborn married Ava Gray on April 19, 1904, and they were the parents of one daughter, Ava Gray (Mrs. B. S. Albritton).

HERBERT DALTON BATEMAN[7]

Herbert Dalton Bateman was born in Washington County on October 21, 1877, son of Richard M. and Sarah Everett Bateman. He attended the public schools in Washington County, Plymouth Academy and then the University of North Carolina.

Mr. Bateman taught school for several years before entering the banking business. From 1903 until 1911 he worked for several banks and then was appointed a state bank examiner, a position he held until 1916, when he came to Branch Banking and Trust Company as cashier. In 1918 he was elected vice president and in 1924 became president. He served in that capacity until his retirement in 1952. He remained a member of the board and served as consultant until his death on August 18, 1956. He was awarded the 50 Year Club membership certificate by the North Carolina Bankers Association in 1953.

Mr. Bateman was a trustee of the Greater University of North Carolina from 1932 until his death. He was a member of the first State Banking Commission, serving from 1937 until 1951. He was also a director of the North Carolina Home Insurance Company, the Reconstruction Finance Corporation of Charlotte and Norfolk Southern Railroad, and he served on the board of stewards of the First Methodist Church.

Mr. Bateman was first married in 1902 to Ida Tucker of Plymouth. They were the parents of three children: Richard H., Ida Louise (Mrs. W.A. McQueen), and Margaret Elizabeth (Mrs. Junius S. Williams) of Fayetteville. Mrs. Bateman died in 1921.

Mr. Bateman married Lottie Skinner Cooper in 1927 and they were the parents of two children: Nell Moseley (Mrs. Lloyd K. Newman) of Norfolk, and Harry Skinner Bateman.

In 1933, two years after the run on the Wilson banks, the State magazine published an article in tribute to him that said, "His methods of running a bank have been tried and have been found worthy." J. E. Paschall, who followed him as president of the bank, said: "His policies and beliefs were not always popular, but he was known in eastern North Carolina … and throughout the state and nation primarily as a man of ability, courage, vision, and integrity who could be depended upon to express his convictions and to live by them, even though others might disagree with his point of view."

Mr. Bateman was selected "Tar Heel of the Week" by the *Raleigh News and Observer* in 1952.

JOSHUA ERNEST PASCHALL[8]

Joshua Ernest Paschall was born in 1896 in Wilson County near Black Creek. The son of Joshua Walter and Sallie Poole Paschall, he was the third of nine children.

Mr. Paschall attended the University of North Carolina and earned a bachelor's degree from Atlantic Christian College and a bachelor of laws degree from American Extension University, Los Angeles. After graduation from Pell's Law School in Rocky Mount, he was admitted to the bar. In 1961 he was awarded an honorary doctor of laws degree by Atlantic Christian College.

Mr. Paschall served as a pharmacist's mate in the Navy during World War I and later was a first lieutenant in the North Carolina National Guard. He was awarded the Cross of Military Service by The John Dunham Chapter, United Daughters of the Confederacy. He was commander of the Robert B. Anderson Post, American Legion, and chef de gare of the Forty and Eight.

Mr. Paschall began his banking career with Branch Banking and Trust Company as a runner and transit clerk in 1919. He was president from 1953 through 1963 and was a member of the board from 1943 until 1972.

Mr. Paschall was elected president of the North Carolina Bankers Association in 1960 and was named to its 50 Year Club in 1969. He served on the State Banking Commission from 1961 until 1965.

After his retirement from the bank, he served three terms as a state representative in the General Assembly from District 15, composed of Wilson and Johnston counties.

Mr. Paschall was a loyal supporter of Atlantic Christian College and the First Christian Church for many years. He was a trustee of the college and president of its Alumni Association. He was chairman of the board of his church for 20 years.

He was president of Wilson Home and Loan Association, the Boy Scouts Court of Honor and the Chamber of Commerce. In addition to county, state and national bar associations, he was a member of the American Judicature Society, National Society of State Legislators, Rotary Club and the Newcomen Society in North America.

Mr. Paschall and his wife, the former Claire Hodges, had two children: Julia Daly (Mrs. Charles W. Mauze) and James Ernest. Mr. Paschall died in Wilson in 1974.

FREDERICK LOUIS CARR[9]

Mr. Carr was born on September 6, 1909, the son of
Frederick Louis Carr, Sr., and Nancy Branch Carr.
His grandfather, Alpheus Branch, founded Branch
Banking and Trust Company in 1872.

He served on the bank's Board of Directors from
1939 until 1979 and was chairman from 1962 until
1979, when he became Board Member Emeritus and
Honorary Chairman. He was a member of the Branch
Corporation Board from 1974 until 1979.

He received his education in the public schools in Wilson,
Fishburne Military Academy and the University of North Carolina, where he
studied law.

Prior to beginning his practice of law, Mr. Carr worked for a year in the Trust
Department of the bank. He was a founder and partner of Carr, Gibbons, Cozart
and Jones, Attorneys, the General Counsel for the bank.

During World War II, Mr. Carr was a Lieutenant Commander in the Navy serving
in the European Theatre.

Mr. Carr was a vestryman of St. Timothy's Episcopal Church and a member of
the bar associations of Wilson County, North Carolina and the United States. He
held key posts in numerous Wilson County charitable and civic associations and
was a member of the Board of Education for five years.

He was married to the late Olivia H. Chamberlain on June 4, 1932. They had one
daughter, Olivia Stuart, and a granddaughter, Susan.

Mr. Carr died on July 19, 1981.

JOHN LAFAYETTE SATCHWELL[10]

John Lafayette Satchwell was president of Branch
Banking and Trust Company from Jan. 1, 1964, until his
retirement on Dec. 31, 1972. He was born in Bath, N.C,
in 1907, the son of John Lafayette Satchwell and
Elizabeth Woolard Satchwell.

The family moved to Washington, N.C., in 1918. After
graduation from high school, he worked a year prior to
entering the University of North Carolina.

Mr. Satchwell began his banking career in 1926 with the First
National Bank of Washington, which closed in 1931 during the Great Depression.
He then went with the Bank of Washington, which he left in 1932 to join the
Goldsboro staff of Branch Banking and Trust Company. Six years later, when
Branch Banking and Trust Company assumed the deposit liabilities of the Bank
of Fremont, he was sent there to manage the Fremont Office and to liquidate the
unassumed assets for the Federal Deposit Insurance Corporation. In 1950 he
transferred to the home office in Wilson as a vice president and was
subsequently promoted to senior vice president and cashier.

Mr. Satchwell was a director of Branch Banking and Trust Company from 1951
until 1977 and a director of Branch Corporation from its formation in 1974 until
1977 when he became board member emeritus of both boards.

Mr. Satchwell held several key posts in the North Carolina Bankers Association
and was recognized by the association in 1976 for 50 years of service to the
banking industry. He also was a director of Dewey Brothers Inc., Goldsboro,
Wilson County Industrial Development Foundation and Wilson County Industrial
Development Corporation. He was a director and member of the executive
committee of the North Carolina Citizens Association.

Local organizations he served included the Chamber of Commerce, where he
was president, the Kiwanis Club, Wilson Industrial Council, Community Chest
and Red Cross. He was the charter president of Fremont Rotary Club and served
on the school board there. He also was a member of The Salvation Army
Advisory Board, Newcomen Society in North America and the Christian Science
Church.

Mr. Satchwell and his wife, the former Elizabeth Rhea Dewey, had one daughter,
Betty Jon (Mrs. Richard T. Smith).

THORNE GREGORY[11]

Thorne Gregory became president of Branch Banking and Trust Company on Jan. 1, 1973. He had been a member of the Board of Directors since 1968 and was elected chairman and chief executive officer of Branch Corporation when it was established in 1974. He held all of these positions until his death in 1982.

Mr. Gregory was born on Dec. 25, 1928, the son of Fletcher Harrison Gregory and Boyd Thorne Gregory of Halifax.

He was a graduate of Fishburne Military School, the University of North Carolina, the North Carolina School of Banking and the Executive Program conducted by the School of Business Administration at UNC.

He joined the Air Force in 1952, and served as a fighter pilot and instructor. He was discharged in 1956 as a first lieutenant.

Mr. Gregory joined the Bank of Halifax in 1956. When that bank merged into Branch Banking and Trust Company in 1968, he was named a vice president and assigned to the Wilson office. In 1969, he transferred to the Raleigh office and was named officer in charge in 1970.

Mr. Gregory served five consecutive two-year terms in the North Carolina House of Representatives and was committee chairman of Federal and Interstate Cooperation, Banks and Banking, Highway Safety and Finance. He was a member of the Advisory Budget Commission, the Governor's Commission on Aviation, the Atlantic States Marine and Fisheries Commission and the North Carolina Board of Higher Education.

Mr. Gregory was elected president of the North Carolina Bankers Association in 1981 and was a member of the executive committee of the North Carolina Citizens Association. He was a board member of the Medical Foundation of North Carolina Inc., the Business Foundation of North Carolina Inc., the Roanoke River Basin Association and Blue Cross and Blue Shield of North Carolina.

While in Raleigh, Mr. Gregory served as a board member of the Rex Hospital Foundation, the Raleigh Chamber of Commerce and Raleigh Merchants Bureau. He also was a member of St. Timothy's Episcopal Church, Kiwanis Club and American Legion.

Mr. Gregory and his wife, the former Hester Lockett, had four children, Hester Elizabeth (Mrs. R. B. Hodde), Boyd Wynns (Mrs. J. K. Dorsett III), Anne Harrison and Thorne, Jr.

GARLAND SCOTT TUCKER, JR.[12]

Garland Scott Tucker, Jr., was born in Raleigh on July 27, 1919, the son of Garland Scott Tucker and Toler Moore Tucker. He attended Raleigh city schools, Virginia Episcopal School in Lynchburg, Virginia, and the University of North Carolina at Chapel Hill.

Mr. Tucker was elected to the board of Branch Banking and Trust Company in February 1954. He became a member of the Executive Committee on July 16, 1957, and served as chairman of that committee from February 4, 1964, until May 23, 1989. He was elected chairman of the board on August 21, 1979, and served in this capacity until March 17, 1987. He was also a member of the Branch Corporation Board from the time it was established in 1974 until his retirement on July 27, 1989, his 70th birthday.

In 1941, while still living in Raleigh, he became associated with G. S. Tucker and Company, a family-owned home furnishings business, and he moved to Wilson the following year. He serves as president of the firm, which has furniture stores located throughout Eastern North Carolina.

Mr. Tucker and the former Jean Smith Barnes of Wilson were married on June 13, 1946. They are the parents of four children: Garland Scott III of Greenwich, Conn., Edwin Davis Barnes of Wilson, Toler Macon (Mrs. Paul Newby) of Raleigh and Sarah Bradshaw (Mrs. Joseph T. Knott III) of Raleigh.

Mr. Tucker has been active in numerous Christian, civic and charitable associations over the years, including West Nash Methodist Church, the Rotary Club and the Salvation Army Advisory Board.

He served as one of the three members of the Finance Committee of Gideons International and has been a member of the 20-member International Cabinet, the governing body of the Gideons International. His responsibilities have included overseeing the distribution of Bibles and Testaments in 41 countries in South America, the Caribbean, Europe and the Near East. He also has been International Chaplain of the Gideons.

L. VINCENT LOWE, JR.[13]

L. Vincent Lowe, Jr., was elected chief executive officer of BB&T and chief executive officer and chairman of BB&T Financial Corporation in 1982. He was elected chairman of BB&T in 1987 and held all these positions until his death in 1989.

Mr. Lowe joined the BB&T Management Development Program in 1961 and was promoted to assistant vice president two years later and named head of the Wallace office. He was vice president in charge of the New Bern office from 1966 to 1970, when he returned to Wilson. He was subsequently named senior vice president and head of the Bank Administration Division, then senior executive vice president and chief operating officer.

Mr. Lowe attended North Carolina State University and graduated from the University of North Carolina at Chapel Hill with a degree in business administration. He earned a certificate from the Stonier Graduate School of Banking at Rutgers and was a graduate of the Executive Management Program of Professional Management Education sponsored by UNC. He served two years of active military service with the U.S. Army assigned to the finance section.

Mr. Lowe became president of the North Carolina Bankers Association in 1989 and was serving in that capacity at the time of his death. He was a trustee of East Carolina University and Atlantic Christian College. He was a member of Robert Morris Associates, the Governor's Business Council on Arts and Humanities, the North Carolina Business Committee for Education and the Medical Foundation of North Carolina Inc. He served as president of The Business Foundation of North Carolina Inc.; vice president of the NCSU Foundation Inc.; and director of North Carolina Citizens for Business and Industry, the Public School Forum of North Carolina Inc., Triangle East and the North Carolina Museum of History Associates.

He also served on the Board of Associates of the North Carolina Child Advocacy Institute, the Board of Trustees of the North Carolina Museum of Art, the board of the Independent College Fund of North Carolina and the Advisory Board of the North Carolina Maritime Museum. He helped organize and served as vice chairman of the board of the Rural Economic Development Center. He also was a member of the First United Methodist Church, where he was chairman of the Administrative Board. Mr. Lowe and his wife, the former Pearla Ann Revelle, had three children, Lester, James and John.

JOHN A. ALLISON IV[14]

John Allison began his service with BB&T in 1971 and managed a wide variety of responsibilities throughout the bank. He became president of BB&T in 1987 and was elected Chairman and CEO in July 1989. During Mr. Allison's tenure as CEO from 1989 to 2008, BB&T grew from $4.5 billion to $152 billion in assets. In March 2009, he joined the faculty of Wake Forest University Schools of Business as Distinguished Professor of Practice.

Allison is a Phi Beta Kappa graduate of the University of North Carolina at Chapel Hill, where he received a B.S. degree in business administration (1971). He received his master's degree in management from Duke University (1974). He is also a graduate of the Stonier Graduate School of Banking and has received Honorary Doctorate Degrees from East Carolina University (1995), Mount Olive College (2002), Clemson University (2005), Marymount University (2008), Mercer University (2009) and Universidad Francisco Marroquin (Guatemala) (2010). Allison received the Corning Award for Distinguished Leadership, was inducted into the N.C. Business Hall of Fame and received the Lifetime Achievement Award from the American Banker in 2009. He was recognized by the Harvard Business Review as one of the top 100 most successful CEOs in the world over the last decade.

He serves on the Wake Forest University Baptist Medical Center Board of Visitors, the Board of Visitors at the Fuqua School of Business at Duke University, the Kenan-Flagler Business School at UNC-Chapel Hill, the Wake Forest University Schools of Business, the Clemson Institute for the Study of Capitalism, and the Mercatus Center at George Mason University. He is also on the Board of Trustees of the Ayn Rand Institute and the Global Transpark Foundation.

Mr. Allison is a past Board member of Guilford College, Barton College, The Financial Services Roundtable, The Clearing House, N.C. Citizens for Business and Industry, the Medical Foundation at East Carolina University, Childrens Services of Eastern N.C. and the Breton Woods Committee.

A native of Charlotte, N.C., Allison is married to the former Elizabeth McDonald of Elkin, N.C. They have two sons and one daughter.

KELLY S. KING

Kelly S. King, a 40-year veteran of BB&T, is chairman, president and chief executive officer of BB&T Corporation. He joined the company's Management Development Program in 1972 and has been a member of its Executive Management team since 1983.

King has held key leadership roles in numerous areas throughout the company, including commercial and retail banking, operations, insurance, corporate financial services, investment services and capital markets. He became president of BB&T Corporation in 1996 and was chief operating officer of BB&T Corporation and Branch Bank from 2004 to 2008.

He has served as president and chief executive officer of BB&T Corporation and chairman and chief executive officer of Branch Bank since 2009 and in 2010 assumed the additional title of chairman of BB&T Corporation. He was named a director of the Federal Reserve Bank of Richmond in 2009.

King has been credited with leading BB&T to continued profitability and financial stability through the economic downturn beginning in 2008. His unwavering commitment to the company's vision, mission and values has led to a nationally recognized employee volunteer program called The Lighthouse Project.

A native of Raleigh, N.C., King received bachelor's and master's degrees in business administration from East Carolina University and also is a graduate of Stonier Graduate School of Banking at Rutgers University.

He is chairman of the Piedmont Triad Partnership and a board member of the Financial Services Roundtable, The Clearing House and Winston-Salem Alliance. He also is a member of the Triangle Community Foundation Leadership Council and the ECU National Leadership Advisory Council.

King has been chairman of the N.C. Bankers Association, N.C. Rural Economic Center, N.C. Small Business and Technology Development Center, Forsyth County United Way Tocqueville Leadership Society and ECU Board of Visitors and served as vice chairman of the American Bankers Council. He also has been an active member, officer and supporter of numerous professional, civic, charitable and educational organizations at both the local and state levels. King is married to Eva Ann King of Washington, N.C. They have two children Mary Ann King and Ken S. King both of Charlotte, N.C.

Biographies of Chairmen
Angus Wilton McLean,
Hector MacLean and
L. Glenn Orr, Jr.
of Southern National

ANGUS WILTON MCLEAN

Angus Wilton McLean founded the Bank of Lumberton in 1897. The bank changed its name to Southern National Bank in 1959.

An industrious Scotsman, McLean also ran a law practice, founded a railroad, started a land development company, created a trust company and built three cotton mills.

In addition, he served as governor of North Carolina, chairman of the N.C. Democratic Party, Undersecretary of the U.S. Treasury and chairman of the War Finance Commission during World War I.

McLean was the oldest child of Robeson County treasurer Archibald Alexander McLean and his wife Caroline Amanda Purcell McLean.

After graduating from McMillian Military Academy in the nearby town of Laurinburg, he taught school to pay his way through the University of North Carolina and UNC Law School.

After earning his law degree, he returned home to Lumberton and opened a law practice. At 27, he founded the Bank of Lumberton and served as its president for more than 37 years. He guided the fledgling bank through the Great Depression and set the standard for leadership in the years to come.

McLean died at age 65, survived by his wife, Margaret, and three children, Angus II, Margaret and Hector.

HECTOR MACLEAN

Hector MacLean, the youngest of Bank of Lumberton founder Angus Wilton McLean's three children, was named president of the National Bank of Lumberton at age 33 after nearly 10 years as a board member and two years as an employee.

MacLean (at age 12, Hector told his father he preferred to use the old Scotch spelling of the family name) worked at a cotton mill in Lumberton as a teenager and considered going into the textile business. He graduated from Davidson College in 1941 and went to Philadelphia – then the center of the textile world – to chase his dream.

But after Pearl Harbor, MacLean's life took a detour. He was drafted into the Army and served in Europe under Gen. George Patton.

After his service in the Army, MacLean enrolled at the University of North Carolina where he earned his undergraduate and law degrees. He practiced law from 1948 to 1952 before joining the National Bank of Lumberton.

MacLean served as mayor of Lumberton from 1949 to 1953. He served as a state senator from Robeson County from 1961 to 1971.

As president of the National Bank of Lumberton, he spearheaded the bank's decision in 1958 to open its first branch outside Robeson County in nearby Laurinburg and changed the bank's name to Southern National Bank.

He guided the bank through its first merger in 1964 with the Bank of Rowland, in the small farming town south of Lumberton, and several mergers to follow in both Carolinas.

MacLean retired as chairman of the board in 1990 after taking Southern National from a corner bank on Elm Street in downtown Lumberton to a statewide, multi-billion-dollar financial institution.

During his 35-year tenure as leader of the bank, assets grew from $11 million to more than $3.3 billion. Deposits grew from $10 million to more than $2.2 billion. The number of branches increased from that single building in Lumberton to 148 branches spread over two states.

MacLean was married to the late Lyl W. MacLean. He has one daughter, Lyl MacLean Clinard.

L. GLENN ORR, JR.

L. Glenn Orr, Jr., former CEO of Forsyth Bank and Trust Company, succeeded Hector MacLean in 1990 as chairman and CEO of Southern National Corporation.

Prior to assuming the chairman's role, Orr served as executive vice president and chairman and CEO of Southern National Bank of North Carolina.

Orr started his banking career as a management trainee at Wachovia in 1966. After eight years, he moved to head the Community Bank of Greenville at age 32.

After one year in Greenville, Orr returned to Winston-Salem, N.C. in 1973 to serve as President and CEO of Forsyth Bank & Trust Co., a position he held until 1982 when Forsyth Bank merged with Southern National.

Orr was at the helm in 1994 when Southern National and BB&T agreed to a merger-of-equals, one of the largest bank mergers in North Carolina history.

Orr is currently chief executive officer of Orr Holdings LLC. He is a life trustee of Wake Forest University in Winston-Salem, N.C. He is a director of Medical Properties Trust, Birmingham, Ala.; Highwoods Properties, Raleigh, N.C.; General Parts Inc., Raleigh, N.C.; Broyhill Management Co. Fund, Lenoir, N.C.; and Old Salem Museums & Gardens, Winston-Salem, N.C. He is the recipient of the "Medallion of Merit" at Wake Forest University.

A Spartanburg native, he is married to the former Ruthlee Phillips of Charlotte, N.C. They have three children, Virginia DeArmon Orr, Laney G. Orr III and Mollie Ruth Orr Britton.

Past and Present
Directors of BB&T

TABLE VII
BB&T Corporation* Board of Directors
as of January 2012
Date represents Election to the Board

John A. Allison IV *1987*
Jennifer S. Banner *2003*
K. David Boyer *2009*
Anna R. Cablik *2004*
Ronald E. Deal *1986*
J. Littleton Glover, Jr. *2009*
Jane P. Helm *1997*
John P. Howe III, M.D. *2005*

Kelly S. King *2008*
Valeria Lynch Lee *2011*
Nido R. Qubein *1990*
Thomas E. Skains *2009*
Thomas N. Thompson *2008*
Edwin H. Welch, Ph.D. *2011*
Steven Taylor Williams *2007*

Past Members of BB&T Corporation
Board of Directors
With dates of Service

Joseph B. Alala, Jr. *1983 – 2003*
W. E. Barnes *1974 – 1981*
William W. Barnes *1981 – 2006*
Paul B. Barringer II *1975 – 2000*
H. S. Bateman *1974 – 1992*
Clifton L. Benson *1983 – 1985*
J. W. Benson *1974 – 1978*
T. F. Bridgers *1974 – 1976*
J. S. Brody *1979 – 1986*
A. Branch Carr *1974 – 1981*
F. L. Carr *1974 – 1979*
Nelle Ratie Chilton *2000 – 2009*
W. G. Clark III *1981 – 2003*
Alfred E. Cleveland *1997 – 2005*
Charles S. Cooke, M. D. *1974 – 1990*
Jesse W. Corbett, Jr. *1981 – 2007*
W. R. Cuthbertson, Jr. *1983 – 2000*
Fred H. Deaton, Jr. *1974 – 2004*
William A. Dees, Jr. *1984 – 1990*
Albert J. Dooley, Sr. *1994 – 2000*
Joe L. Dudley, Sr. *1992 – 1997*
J. C. Eagles, Jr. *1974 – 1980*
Tom D. Efird *1981 – 2009*
O. William Fenn, Jr. *1991 – 1997*
Barry J. Fitzpatrick *2003 – 2010*
E. Thomas Franklin *1977 – 1984*
Paul S. Goldsmith *1970 – 2003*
John Graves *1974 – 1990*
Fletcher H. Gregory, Jr. *1974 – 1987*
Thorne Gregory *1974 – 1982*
L. Vincent Hackley, Ph.D. *1992 – 2010*
Ernest F. Hardee *1995 – 1997*
James E. "Buddy" Heins *1985 – 2000*
J. Mack Holland *1982 – 1983*
Richard Janeway, M. D. *1989 – 2003*
Raymond A. Jones *1974 – 1994*
K. D. Kennedy *1974 – 1983*
David R. Lafar III *1990 – 1994*
Ted B. Lanier *1985 – 1986*

J. Ernest Lathem, M.D. *1987 – 2004*
James L. Lee *1974 – 1980*
L. Vincent Lowe, Jr. *1974 – 1989*
James H. Maynard *1985 – 2010*
Joseph A. McAleer *1993 – 2002*
Albert O. McCauley *1993 – 2010*
James Dickson McLean, Jr. *1956 – 1997*
Nathan McElwee *1974 – 1979*
J. Irvin Morgan, Jr. *1974 – 1980*
J. Holmes Morrison *2000 – 2011*
Albert G. Myers, Jr. *1982 – 1987*
Charles E. Nichols *1984 – 1997*
L. Glen Orr, Jr. *1982 – 1997*
W. H. Parks *1987 – 1993*
Plato Pearson, Jr. *1982 – 1986*
A. Winniett Peters *1977 – 1997*
Richard L. Player, Jr. *1990 – 2004*
C. Edward Pleasants, Jr. *1993 – 2004*
Paul B. Porter *1982 – 1990*
E. Rhone Sasser *1997 – 2007*
J. L. Satchwell *1974 – 1977*
Ralph R. Schmidt *1987 – 1993*
Jack E. Shaw *1997 – 2004*
Will Carr Smith *1974 – 1983*
B. Gloyden Stewart, Jr. *1974 – 1982*
George T. Stronach *1974 – 1977*
S. B. Tanner III *1982 – 1994*
J. Marshall Tetterton *1974 – 1976*
Garland S. Tucker *1974 – 1989*
Larry J. Waggoner *1985 – 2002*
R. P. Watson Jr. *1974 – 1978*
Harold B. Wells *1997 – 2001*
Clarence W. Wickham *1980 – 1984*
A. Tab Williams, Jr. *1982 – 1997*
Henry G. Williamson, Jr. *1986 – 2004*
Samuel J. Wornom III *1985 – 1991*
Albert S. Wylie *1974 – 1981*
William B. Young, M. D. *1974 – 1995*
Albert F. Zettlemoyer *2003 – 2005*

* Branch Corporation was changed to BB&T Financial Corporation in 1988. The name was changed again to Southern National Corporation when the bank merged with Southern National Corporation on February 28, 1995. Southern National was renamed BB&T Corporation on May 16, 1997.

TABLE VIII
Branch Banking and Trust Company Board* of Directors
as of January 2012
Date represents Election to the Board

James A. Faulkner *2001*
Thomas K. Ferguson *1999*
I. Pat Henry *1999*
Eric C. Kendrick *2003*
Kelly S. King *1995*
Louis B. Lynn *2007*

Edward C. Milligan *2006*
Donald N. Patten *2006*
Charles A. Patton *1998*
Tollie W. Rich, Jr. *2006*
David W. Smith, Jr. *2006*

Past Members of Branch Banking and Trust Company
Board of Directors
With dates of Service

J.W. Adams *1997 – 2000*
Joseph B. Alala, Jr. *1983 – 2003*
John A. Allison IV *1986 – 2009*
G. Robert Aston, Jr. *1995 – 1997*
Albert Anderson *1903 – 1909*
H. W. Anderson *1940 – 1950*
S. W. Anderson *1936 – 1953*
John Van Ness Andrews *1997 – 2004*
Phyllis H. Arnold *2000 – 2011*
William C. Ballard *2004 – 2007*
W. L. Banks *1904 – 1917*
George T. Barnes *1956 – 1973*
J. N. Barnes *1936 – 1937*
John T. Barnes *1917 – 1934*
W. E. Barnes *1974 – 1981*
W. Watson Barnes, Sr. *1980 – 2006*
Paul B. Barringer *1974 – 1995*
Nathan Bass *1911 – 1913*
H. D. Bateman *1917 – 1956*
Clifton L. Benson *1983 – 1985*
J. W. Benson *1968 – 1978*
D. S. Boykin *1903 – 1941*
Robert L. Brady *1991 – 2000*
F. N. Bridgers *1917 – 1956*
T. F. Bridgers *1956 – 1976*
R. G. Bridgers *1903 – 1911*
William F. Black *1995 – 2000*
Kenneth E. Boring *2000 – 2003*
J. S. Brody *1979 – 1986*
Thomas R. Brumbley *2007 – 2009*
T. F. Bridgers *1974 – 1976*
John A. Campbell, Jr. *1956 – 1973*
A. Branch Carr *1958 – 1981*
B. W. Carr *1937 – 1956*
C. Stuart Carr, Jr. *1951 – 1956*
F. L. Carr, Sr. *1909 – 1939*
F. L. Carr *1939 – 1979*
W. G. Carr *1911 – 1930*
W. E. Carter *1997 – 2009*
Russell M. Carter *1997 – 2000*

Raymond S. Caughman *1994 – 1995*
J. T. Cheatham *1920 – 1947*
W. G. Clark III *1980 – 2003*
James L. Clayton *2001 – 2004*
Alfred E. Cleveland *1997 – 2005*
G. W. Connor *1903 – 1913*
H. G. Connor *1903 – 1907*
H. G. Connor, Jr. *1915 – 1917*
Jesse W. Corbett, Jr. *1980 – 2007*
James L. Cresimore *1997 – 2000*
E. B. Crow *1943 – 1974*
F. Shelby Cullom *1954 – 1960*
E. A. Darden *1903 – 1930*
J. D. Dawes *1903 – 1914*
John B. Deans *1903 – 1917*
Fred H. Deaton, Jr. *1971 – 2001*
Thomas P. Dillon *1997 – 1998*
Joe L. Dudley, Sr. *1992 – 1998*
J. C. Eagles, Jr. *1952 – 1980*
Tom D. Efird *1981 – 1995*
R. Marshall Evans *2007 – 2011*
O. William Fenn, Jr. *1991 – 1997*
B. G. Field *1943 – 1961*
Harry C. Finch *1954 – 1959*
W. A. Finch *1920 – 1941*
Andrew S. Fine *1995 – 1997*
Robert R. Fowler III *2006 – 2008*
E. Thomas Franklin *1976 – 1984*
C. M. "Bill" Gatton *2002 – 2004*
Major General L. H. Ginn III *2002 – 2005*
J. Littleton Glover, Jr. *1999 – 2010*
Miley C. Glover *1934 – 1935*
E. B. Graves *1903 – 1904*
John Graves *1958 – 1990*
Fletcher H. Gregory, Jr. *1968 – 1987*
Thorne Gregory *1968 – 1982*
Robert E. Greene *1995 – 2006*
Thorne Gregory *1974 – 1982*
L. Vincent Hackley, Ph.D. *1992 – 2010*

* Branch Corporation was changed to BB&T Financial Corporation in 1988. The name was changed again to Southern National Corporation when the bank merged with Southern National Corporation on February 28, 1995. Southern National was renamed BB&T Corporation on May 16, 1997.

TABLE VIII
Past Members of Branch Banking and Trust Company
Board of Directors *(continued)*
With dates of Service

J. C. Hadley *1913 – 1913*
J. C. Hales *1903 – 1913*
Robert F. Hatcher *1999 – 2006*
Ernest R. Hardee *1995 – 1998*
James A. Hardison, Jr. *1995 – 2000*
C. L. Hardy *1930 – 1950*
James E. Heins *1984 – 2000*
James C. High *1997 – 2003*
S. E. High, Jr. *1964 – 1970*
Donald C. Hiscott *1987 – 2002*
J. Mack Holland *1981 – 1983*
Raymond A. Jones, Jr. *1974 – 1994*
K. D. Kennedy *1958 – 1983*
Kelly S. King *1995 – 2009*
William R. Klich *2004 – 2006*
David R. LaFar III *1990 – 1994*
B. F. Lane *1903 – 1909*
H. B. Lane *1911 – 1941*
J. J. Lane *1935 – 1966*
S. S. Lawrence *1928 – 1972*
James L. Lee *1967 – 1980*
Valeria Lynch-Lee *2002 – 2010*
A. Patrick Linton *2001 – 2004*
L. Vincent Lowe, Jr. *1979 – 1989*
James Maynard *1984 – 1985*
Nathan McElwee *1971 – 1979*
A. D. McGowan *1919 – 1920*
James Dickerson McLean, Jr. *1956 – 1997*
S. G. Mewborn *1915 – 1937*
J. Irvin Morgan, Jr. *1951 – 1980*
L. A. Moye *1948 – 1972*
H. H. Murray *1910 – 1915*
Albert G. Myers, Jr. *1981 – 1987*
Charles E. Nichols *1984 – 1997*
C. E. Moore, M.D. *1903 – 1941*
Dan R. Moore *1999 – 2010*
J. Irvin Morgan, Jr. *1951 – 1980*
H. H. Murray *1910 – 1915*
L. Glenn Orr, Jr. *1982 – 1997*

Dorothy G. Owen *1992 – 1994*
J. E. Paschall *1943 – 1972*
Alvis Patterson *1915 – 1917*
Plato Pearson, Jr. *1981 – 1986*
Darrell D. Pittard *2001 – 2002*
E. B. Pittman *1958 – 1974*
Paul B. Porter *1981 – 1990*
J. G. Raper *1915 – 1924*
Kenneth H. Rayborn *2006 – 2007*
Theodore R. Reynolds *1988 – 2002*
W. R. Rodgers *1960 – 1969*
E. Rhone Sasser *1997 – 2007*
J. L. Satchwell *1951 – 1977*
W. E. P. Sharpe *1905 – 1936*
Jack E. Shaw *1997 – 2004*
R. B. Simpson *1915 – 1916*
Will Carr Smith *1956 – 1983*
E. W. Staples *1920 – 1927*
B. Gloyden Stewart, Jr. *1974 – 1982*
George T. Stronach *1968 – 1977*
S. B. Tanner III *1981 – 1994*
J. Marshall Tetterton *1974 – 1976*
Thomas N. Thompson *2006 – 2008*
Garland S. Tucker, Jr. *1954 – 1989*
Larry J. Waggoner *1985 – 2001*
R. P. Watson *1920 – 1932*
R. P. Watson, Jr. *1934 – 1978*
R. S. Wells *1903 – 1905*
G. H. Whitehead *1903 – 1911*
Clarence W. Wickham *1980 – 1984*
A. Bruce Williams, Jr. *1982 – 1997*
Jesse B. Williams *1903 – 1904*
Henry G. Williamson, Jr. *1986 – 2003*
Charles M. Winston *1997 – 2000*
Alfred B. Whitt *2001 – 2008*
P. L. Woodard *1917 – 1923*
Samuel J. Wornam III *1984 – 1991*
Albert S. Wylie *1979 – 1981*
William B. Young, M.D. *1967 – 1995*

* Branch Corporation was changed to BB&T Financial Corporation in 1988. The name was changed again to Southern National Corporation when the bank merged with Southern National Corporation on February 28, 1995. Southern National was renamed BB&T Corporation on May 16, 1997.

Appendix

TABLE IX
BB&T State Banks

Past Members of BB&T of South Carolina Board of Directors*
Date represents Election to the Board

Charles F. Ailstock *1988*	Harvey Graham, Jr. *1989*
James H. Benson, Jr. *1997*	Kelly S. King *1991*
Luther C. Boliek *1994*	Reamer B. King *1988*
Robert Bouknight *2001*	J. Ernest Lathem, M. D. *1987*
Michael R. Brenan *1999*	Robert Livingston *1999*
Vasa W. Cate, M.D. *1995*	Louis B. Lynn, Ph.D. *2003*
Harry Chapman, Jr. *1973*	John J. Martin, Jr. *1976*
Henry Clinkscales *1987*	Thurmon W. McLamb *1986*
Merl F. Code *1997*	T. Travis Medlock *1995*
Howard W. Covington, Jr. *1997*	Billy Painter *2001*
Phyllis Buchheit DeLapp *2000*	Jerry Stanaland *1986*
Curtis Dickerson *1987*	Heywood M. Sulliva *1994*
Robert N. Hubbs *1995*	J. Rutledge Young, Jr. *1988*
Caroline Sawyer Glover *2001*	

* Dissolved in 2006.

Past Members of BB&T Virginia Board of Directors*
Date represents Election to the Board

Sally James Andrews *1990*	Edward M. Holland *2003*
W. Christopher Beeler, Jr. *1999*	Bob M. Johnson *2000*
Charles Blankenship *2003*	William Jonak, Jr. *2000*
Edward L. Breeden III *1999*	Kelly S. King *1998*
Fraiser W. Brickhouse *1998*	Frank E. Laughon, Jr. *1998*
James K. Candler *2000*	Gerald L. Martin *1998*
J.W. Whiting Chrisman, Jr. *1986*	Richard J. November *1998*
William Lee Cooper III *1999*	Donald N. Patten *1998*
Preston H. Cottrell *1998*	Charles A. Patton *1998*
Barry D. Crawford *1998*	William A. Patton *1999*
Ed Cunningham *1998*	W. Lee Phillips *2005*
Charles E. Curtis *2001*	H. R. Pollard IV *1998*
James L. Davidson, Jr. *2000*	Tollie W. Rich, Jr. *1998*
Elwood L. Edwards *1986*	David C. Smith *1998*
Ronald M. Evins *1998*	Linda Vickers-Smith *1998*
William Eure *2000*	George Vakos *2001*
Berkwood M. Farmer, Ph.D. *1998*	Ralph C. Ward *1998*
Barry J. Fitzpatrick *1998*	Robert G. Watts *2002*
Donald Fentres *2000*	Alfred B. Whitt *2001*
Paul H. Geithner, Jr. *2005*	John H. Wick III *2000*
Benjamin S. Gill *1998*	F. Lewis Wood *1986*
Henry O. Harris III *2004*	Robert H. Zalokar *2005*
John C. Harry III *1990*	

* Dissolved in 2006.

Past Members of BB&T West Virginia* Board of Directors
Date represents Election to the Board

Phyllis H. Arnold *1988*
Charles M. Avampato *1984*
Nelle Ratrie Chilton *1989*
R. Marshall Evans, Jr. *1984*
Robert E. Kamm, Jr. *1986*
John D. Lynch *1986*
Edward H. Maier *1981*
J. Holmes Morrison *1990*

Dan R. Moore *2001*
Charles R. Neighborgall *1993*
William A. Rice, Jr. *1995*
Brent Robinson *1985*
Richard B. Walker *1991*
Edwin H. Welch, Ph.D. *1998*
John H. Wick III *1990*

*Dissolved in 2006.

Past Members of BB&T Georgia* Board of Directors
Date represents Election to the Board

James M. Boring *2000*
Kenneth Boring *2000*
Anna Cablik *2001*
Robert Candler *2000*
Steven S. Dunlevie *2000*
R. Marshall Evans, Jr. *2000*

James A. Faulkner *2001*
J. Littleton Glover, Jr. *2000*
Robert F. Hatcher *2000*
Alfred R. Kennickell, Jr. *2000*
Darrell Pittard *2000*
H. M. Ponder, Jr. *2000*

*Dissolved in 2006.

Past Members of BB&T Kentucky* Board of Directors
Date represents Election to the Board

Anthony G. Bittel, Jr. *2000*
Thomas R. Brumbley *1982*
James E. Cain *1996*
Governor, Martha Layne Collins *1988*
Cecile W. Garmon *1994*
Raymond Kendrick Guillaume *1995*

Terry B. Mobley *2000*
Preston P. Nunnelly *1990*
Rakesh Sachdeva *2003*
David W. Smith, Jr. *1986*
Thomas N. Thompson *1986*
Damon S. Vitale *1996*

*Dissolved in 2006.

TABLE X
BB&T Banking Offices

Beginning in 1872 with the first banking office in Wilson, N.C., BB&T has steadfastly expanded its footprint outside of its home state. Acquisitions in 1986 added offices in South Carolina. A robust pace of acquisitions in the 1990s added additional financial centers in Virginia, Maryland, Washington, D.C., Georgia and West Virginia. Beginning in 2000, BB&T extended its presence by acquisitions in Tennessee, Kentucky, Indiana and Florida. The decade culminated with the FDIC-assisted purchase of Colonial Bank of Alabama resulting in the addition of Texas to the banking marketplace. In January 2012 BB&T bank subsidiaries operated approximately 1,800 financial centers.

TABLE XI
Selected Financial Data
(In Thousands)

Date	Total Assets	Investment Securities	Loans	Total Deposits	Shareholders' Equity
February 18, 1898	$ 270	$ 2	$ 207	$ 204	$ 66
December 2, 1899	300		247	219	72
December 24, 1900	353		260	259	74
September 30, 1901	373	1	259	267	76
November 25, 1902	454	2	301	371	81
November 17, 1903	488	1	358	345	132
September 6, 1904	539	1	439	287	133
November 9, 1905	607	2	449	436	139
November 12, 1906	578	2	447	408	143
December 3, 1907	632	2	500	406	146
November 27, 1908	574	2	464	399	151
December 14, 1909	674	10	469	471	151
December 17, 1910	788	10	575	585	151
December 11, 1911	797	36	609	575	154
December 21, 1912	1,248	57	885	1,083	166
December 8, 1913	1,186	53	920	983	178
December 8, 1914	1,067	51	788	796	176
December 10, 1915	1,109	56	836	932	177
December 27, 1916	1,735	133	1,032	1,551	184
December 31, 1917	2,168	161	1,421	1,984	184
December 31, 1918	2,597	245	1,543	2,409	188
December 31, 1919	4,879	21	3,375	4,684	194
December 29, 1920	2,879	322	2,324	1,846	533
December 31, 1921	2,743	45	2,028	2,133	546
December 29, 1922	3,366	150	2,471	2,762	550
December 31, 1923	4,347	383	2,855	3,779	552
December 31, 1924	3,466	1,468	1,553	2,910	556
December 31, 1925	3,836	1,499	1,575	3,165	591
December 31, 1926	4,273	1,809	1,554	3,671	602
December 31, 1927	5,549	2,497	1,977	4,902	647
December 31, 1928	4,993	1,817	2,549	4,323	670
December 31, 1929	4,725	1,226	2,612	4,039	686
December 31, 1930	5,427	1,497	2,545	4,724	695
December 31, 1931	6,386	2,270	2,515	5,128	694
December 31, 1932	7,695	3,627	2,168	7,004	676
December 31, 1933	13,773	8,301	1,976	12,630	1,041
December 31, 1934	19,040	13,618	2,325	17,678	1,254
December 31, 1935	20,057	12,739	1,614	18,392	1,400
December 31, 1936	19,906	13,671	2,031	18,043	1,596
December 31, 1937	22,248	14,417	2,216	20,256	1,678
December 31, 1938	21,539	13,902	2,371	19,449	1,765
December 31, 1939	24,710	14,926	2,364	22,723	1,621
December 31, 1940	24,215	14,316	2,858	22,172	1,678
December 31, 1941	32,729	18,654	2,973	30,652	1,710
December 31, 1942	60,560	45,670	2,198	58,444	1,743
December 31, 1943	63,789	49,822	2,838	61,503	1,782
December 31, 1944	97,763	74,583	3,516	95,409	1,842
December 31, 1945	107,432	89,702	2,733	104,925	1,933
December 31, 1946	113,440	86,887	3,641	110,882	1,994
December 31, 1947	109,461	76,842	5,342	106,870	2,104
December 31, 1948	97,049	69,868	5,597	94,111	2,233
December 31, 1949	95,949	69,709	6,518	89,373	5,457
December 31, 1950	99,508	69,156	8,118	92,617	5,771
December 31, 1951	124,942	90,429	10,094	117,690	6,131
December 31, 1952	121,499	84,529	12,447	113,645	6,648
December 31, 1953	124,055	84,155	14,428	115,700	8,067
December 31, 1954	117,842	74,337	15,774	108,525	8,586
December 31, 1955	116,757	50,587	39,693	107,393	9,026

Date	Total Assets	Investment Securities	Loans	Total Deposits	Shareholders' Equity
December 31, 1956	108,701	46,564	30,669	98,675	9,623
December 31, 1957	100,564	51,587	25,332	89,799	10,428
December 31, 1958	111,432	64,030	25,293	99,054	11,241
December 31, 1959	110,719	46,048	40,383	97,975	11,932
December 31, 1960	120,411	57,341	40,562	106,776	12,549
December 31, 1961	130,234	63,409	43,191	115,116	13,686
December 31, 1962	148,845	66,562	50,360	130,514	16,757
December 31, 1963	145,805	63,172	53,332	124,666	17,222
December 31, 1964	153,392	61,050	68,839	133,358	17,699
December 31, 1965	162,570	60,851	71,686	140,505	18,241
December 31, 1966	171,872	63,512	82,226	150,001	18,682
December 31, 1967	197,907	75,929	91,317	171,280	20,847
December 31, 1968	230,106	79,228	112,086	201,182	23,464
December 31, 1969	247,435	77,246	131,980	213,009	24,409
December 31, 1970	280,290	70,624	155,290	240,947	26,853
December 31, 1971	305,567	70,391	174,730	263,123	27,828
December 31, 1972	343,567	77,169	200,835	298,792	28,469
December 31, 1973	388,765	92,329	227,999	338,697	29,980
December 31, 1974	410,359	94,079	234,547	352,377	32,005
December 31, 1975	429,294	136,884	214,727	378,527	35,153
December 31, 1976	465,162	140,898	239,723	420,748	39,982
December 31, 1977	504,035	107,127	292,516	455,575	42,771
December 31, 1978	544,852	126,443	328,692	488,910	46,456
December 31, 1979	601,575	129,200	381,237	533,201	51,152
December 31, 1980	714,812	168,953	437,611	625,062	60,339
December 31, 1981	1,133,584	341,776	646,817	965,002	92,613
December 31, 1982	1,368,222	386,430	815,060	1,163,809	97,903
December 31, 1983	1,706,961	376,117	1,133,292	1,443,791	117,369
December 31, 1984	2,383,893	526,922	1,540,707	2,306,858	157,002
December 31, 1985	2,765,684	783,323	1,713,814	2,226,330	175,447
December 31, 1986*	3,281,080	789,619	2,099,053	2,687,445	205,448
December 31, 1987**	3,984,281	887,531	2,626,709	3,136,435	249,553
December 31, 1988***	4,376,600	976,346	3,030,186	3,551,788	277,980
December 31, 1989***	4,807,836	1,052,249	3,195,304	3,899,428	311,051
December 31, 1990***	5,158,726	1,257,751	3,423,810	4,406,442	375,506
December 31, 1991***	6,229,014	1,585,935	4,233,429	5,203,499	486,502
December 31, 1992***	6,691,484	1,725,014	4,524,665	5,346,320	560,908
December 31, 1993***	9,173,117	2,200,813	6,306,443	6,995,121	743,512
December 31, 1994***	10,394,330	2,471,438	7,199,569	7,520,324	822,644
December 31, 1995****	20,492,929	5,355,313	13,812,485	14,684,056	1,674,063
December 31, 1996****	21,246,562	5,261,507	14,584,064	14,953,914	1,729,169
December 31, 1997*****	29,177,600	6,697,192	20,289,955	20,210,116	2,237,637
December 31, 1998	34,427,227	8,159,266	23,694,776	23,046,907	2,758,548
December 31, 1999	43,481,000	10,672,000	29,197,000	27,251,000	3,199,000
December 31, 2000	59,340,000	13,948,000	40,301,000	38,015,000	4,786,000
December 31, 2001	70,870,000	16,760,000	47,443,000	44,733,000	6,150,000
December 31, 2002	80,217,000	17,803,000	53,518,000	51,280,000	7,388,000
December 31, 2003	90,467,000	16,317,000	62,305,000	59,350,000	9,935,000
December 31, 2004	100,509,000	19,173,000	68,163,000	67,699,000	10,874,000
December 31, 2005	109,170,000	20,489,000	75,023,000	74,282,000	11,129,000
December 31, 2006	121,351,000	22,868,000	83,591,000	80,971,000	11,745,000
December 31, 2007	132,618,000	23,428,000	91,686,000	86,766,000	12,632,000
December 31, 2008	152,015,000	33,219,000	98,669,000	98,613,000	16,037,000
December 31, 2009	165,764,000	34,545,000	106,207,000	114,965,000	16,241,000
December 31, 2010	157,081,000	23,169,000	107,264,000	107,213,000	16,498,000
December 31, 2011	174,579,000	36,407,000	111,205,000	124,939,000	17,480,000

* Branch Corporation and wholly owned subsidiary,
  Branch Banking and Trust Company. Years prior to 1974,
  Branch Banking and Trust Company.
** Includes totals for Branch Corporation of South Carolina.

*** BB&T Financial Corporation and subsidiaries.
**** Includes totals for BB&T Financial Corporation and Southern
  National Corporation following their merger of equals on February 28, 1995.
***** Includes UCB on July 1, 1997.

TABLE XII
The Rank (in deposits) of Branch Banking and Trust Company in the Top 300 Banks of the Country
as Compiled by *The American Banker.*

Date	Rank	Date	Rank
1933	259	1962	265
1934	244	1963	277
1935	262	1964	282
1936	295	1965	289
1937	266	1966	282
1938	284	1967	276
1939	270	1968	252
1940	298	1969	248
1941	262	1970	244
1942	187	1971	260
1943	213	1972	262
1944	172	1973	253
1945	186	1974	247
1946	159	1975	246
1947	172	1976	236
1948	191	1977	244
1949	208	1978	251
1950	215	1979	251
1951	178	1980	235
1952	196	1981	170
1953	199	1982	160
1954	214	1983	146
1955	224	1984	117
1956	247	1985	119
1957	280	1986	109
1958	274	1987	110*
1959	281	1988	104*
1960	268	1989	103*
1961	264	1990	113*
		1991	101*

* Represents BB&T of N.C. only.

TABLE XIII
Asset Ranking of BB&T Corporation
Among the Top 100 Bank Holding Companies in the U.S.
Source: *The American Banker.*

Date	Rank		Date	Rank	
1989	96		1995	35	
1990	93		1996	36	
1991	80		1997	32	
1992	78		1998	26	
1993	65		1999*	21	*Q1 2000
1994	61		2000	18	
1995	35		2001*	16	*Q2 2002
1996	36		2002	16	
1997	32		2003	16	
1998	26		2004	13	
1989	96		2005	13	
1990	93		2006*	14	*Q1 2007
1991	80		2007	16	
1992	78		2008	12	
1993	65		2009	14	
1994	61		2010	15	
			2011	16	

Rankings exclude foreign BHCs

TABLE XIV
BB&T Mergers and Acquisitions
Banks and Thrifts

Company	Location	Date
Toisnot Banking Company	Elm City, NC	1931
Wilson Industrial Bank	Wilson,NC	1958
Planters Bank	Stantonsburg, NC	1959
Citizens Bank	Princeton, NC	1961
Bank of Rowland	Rowland, NC	1964
The Farmers Bank & Trust Company	Rockingham, NC	1965
The National Bank of Sanford	Sanford, NC	1965
First National Bank of Leaksville	Eden, NC	1966
First National Bank of Whiteville	Whiteville, NC	1966
Bank of Davie	Mocksville, NC	1967
Bank of Mayodan	Madison, NC	1967
The Bank of Mount Gilead	Mount Gilead, NC	1967
Bank of Halifax	Halifax, NC	1968
First National Bank in Henderson	Henderson, NC	1968
Bank of Varina	Fuquay-Varina, NC	1969
Bank of Charlotte	Charlotte, NC	1970
Bank of Statesville	Statesville, NC	1970
Wilson County Bank and Trust	Wilson, NC	1974
Bank of Matthews	Matthews, NC	1976
Citizens of Warrenton	Warrenton, NC	1976
Lafayette Bank	Fayetteville, NC	1977
Carolina State Bank	Gastonia, NC	1979
Edgecombe Bank & Trust	Tarboro, NC	1980
Independence National Bank	Gastonia, NC	1981
Forsyth Bank and Trust Company	Winston-Salem, NC	1982
City National Bank	Charlotte, NC	1983
Carolina Bancorp	Sanford, NC	1984
Cherryville National Bank	Cherryville, NC	1984
Community Bank of Carolina	Greensboro, NC	1984
The First National Bank of Anson County	Wadesboro, NC	1984
Capital Bank and Trust	Belton, SC	1986
Community Bank Corporation	Greenville, SC	1987
First Palmetto Bancshares Corporation	Columbia, SC	1986
Horry County National Bank	Loris, SC	1986
Liberty National Bank	Charleston, SC	1987
The Union National Bank of Oxford	Oxford, NC	1987
American Bank & Trust Company	High Point, NC	1989
First Federal of Pitt County	Greenville, NC	1990
First Federal of the Carolinas	High Point, NC	1990
Mutual Federal Savings and Loan	Elkin, NC	1990
Western Carolina Savings and Loan	Valdese, NC	1990
Albemarle Savings & Loan Assoc.	Elizabeth City, NC	1991
Gate City Federal	Greensboro, NC	1991
Home Savings & Loan Association	Durham, NC	1991
Preferred Savings Bank	High Point, NC	1991
Southeastern Federal Savings Bank	Charlotte, NC	1991
Workmen's Federal Savings Bank	Mount Airy,NC	1992
First Security Savings and Loan	Pinehurst,NC	1992
Peoples Federal Savings Bank	Thomasville, NC	1992
1st Home Federal	Winston-Salem, NC	1993

Company	Location	Date
Carolina Savings Bank	Wilmington,NC	1993
Citizens Savings Bank (Mooresville)	Mooresville,NC	1993
Citizens Savings Bank (Newton)	Newton,NC	1993
East Coast Savings Bank	Goldsboro,NC	1993
Edenton Savings & Loan Assoc.	Edenton,NC	1993
FedFirst Bancshares	Winston-Salem, NC	1993
First Financial Savings Bank	Kinston, NC	1993
Mutual Savings Bank/Rockingham	Reidsville, NC	1993
Old Stone Bank of NC	Highpoint, NC	1993
Security Federal Savings Bank	Durham, NC	1993
Home Federal Savings Bank	Statesville, NC	1993
LSB Bancshares (South Carolina)	Lexington, SC	1994
Regency Bancshares	Hickory, NC	1994
The First	Greenville, SC	1994
BB&T / SNC	Wilson / Winston, NC	1995
Commerce Bank (Virginia)	Virginia Beach, VA	1995
Fidelity Financial (Virginia)	Richmond, VA	1996
United Carolina Bank	Whiteville, NC	1997
Virginia First Financial Corporation	Petersburg, VA	1997
Franklin Bancorporation	Washington, D.C.	1998
Life Bancorp	Norfolk, VA	1998
Maryland Federal Bancorp	Hyattsville, MD	1998
MainStreet Bank	Martinsville, VA	1999
First Citizens Corporation	Newnan, GA	1999
Mason-Dixon Bancshares, Inc.	Westminster, MD	1999
Matewan BankShares Inc.	Williamson, WV	1999
First Liberty Financial Corp.	Macon, GA	1999
Premier Bancshares, Inc.	Atlanta, GA	2000
Hardwick Holding Company	Dalton, GA	2000
First Banking Company of S.E. Georgia	Statesboro, GA	2000
One Valley Bancorp, Inc.	Charleston, WV	2000
FCNB Corp	Frederick, MD	2000
BankFirst Corporation	Knoxville, TN	2000
FirstSpartan Financial Corp	Spartanburg, SC	2001
Century South Banks, Inc.	Alpharetta, GA	2001
F&M National Corporation	Winchester, VA	2001
Virginia Capital Bancshares	Fredericksburg, VA	2001
Community First Banking Company	Carrollton, GA	2001
Area Bancshares	Owensboro, KY	2001
MidAmerica Banccorp	Louisville, KY	2001
Regional Financial Corporation	Tallahassee, FL	2002
Equitable Bank	Wheaton, MD	2002
First Virginia Banks, Inc.	Falls Church, VA	2003
Republic Bancshares, Inc.	St. Petersburg, FL	2003
Main Street Banks, Inc.	Atlanta, G	2005
First Citizens Bancorp	Cleveland, TN	2006
Coastal Financial Corporation	Myrtle Beach, SC	2007
Haven Trust Bank (FDIC Assisted)	Duluth, GA	2008
Colonial Bank (FDIC Assisted)	Montgomery, AL	2009

TABLE XV
Southern National Mergers and Acquisitions

Company	Location	Date
Bank of Rowland	Rowland, NC	1964
Farmers Bank and Trust	Rockingham, NC	1965
National Bank of Sanford	Sanford, NC	1965
	Lillington, NC	1965
First National of Whiteville	Whiteville, NC	1966
	Tabor City, NC	1966
	Chadbourn, NC	1966
First National of Leaksville	Leaksville (now Eden, NC)	1967
	Spray, NC	
Bank of Mayodan	Mayodan, NC	1967
Bank of Mt. Gilead	Mt. Gilead, NC	1967
First National of Henderson	Henderson, NC	1968
Bank of Varina	Fuquay-Varina, NC	1969
Unifed Investors Life Insurance Co.	Lumberton, NC	1969
Bank of Charlotte	Charlotte, NC	1970
Interstate Leasing	Charlotte, NC	1974
Marvin Greene Mortgage	Charlotte, NC	1974
Lafayette Bank	Fayetteville, NC	1977
Carolina State Bank	Gastonia, NC	1979
Branch Bank of NCNB	Goldsboro, NC	1979
Forsyth Bank and Trust	Winston-Salem, NC	1982
Community Bank of Carolina	Greensboro, NC	1984
First National Bank of Anson County	Wadesboro, NC	1984
	Lilesville, NC	
	Morven, NC	
Cherryville National	Cherryville, NC	1984
Branch of First Union	Hickory, NC	1986
Branch of First Union	Statesville, NC	1986
Horry County National Bank	Loris, SC	1986
Capital Bank and Trust	Belton, SC	1986
First Palmetto Bancshares Corporation	Columbia, SC	1986
Liberty National Bank	Charleston, SC	1987
The Union National Bank of Oxford	Oxford, NC	1987
American Bank and Trust Company	High Point, NC	1989
Mutual Federal Savings and Loan	Elkin, NC	1990
Western Carolina Savings and Loan	Valdese, NC	1990
Southeastern Federal Savings Bank	Charlotte, NC	1991
Preferred Savings Bank	High Point, NC	1991
Workmen's Federal Savings Bank	Mount Airy, NC	1992
First Security Savings Bank	Pinehurst, NC	1992
FedFirst Bancshares	Winston-Salem, NC	1993
First Savings Bank of Greenville	Greenville, SC	1993

TABLE XVI
BB&T Insurance Acquisitions

Company	Location	Date
An Independent Insurance Agency	Wilson, NC	1922
Unified Investors Life Insurance Company	Phoenix, AZ	1969
A&A Agency	Asheville, NC	1987
Ervin, Haywood & Rankin	High Point, NC	1988
Westbrook, Norton, Keesler & Stanley	Charlotte, NC	1989
Cline-Southern	Hickory, NC	1989
Wright, Dobbins, Farnam Associates, Inc.	Asheville, NC	1991
Regional Insurance Services	Sanford, NC	1992
Gouger, O'Neal & Saunders	Aberdeen, NC	1992
West Insurance	Fayetteville, NC	1993
Wilkinson, Bulluck and Company	Rocky Mount, NC	1993
Ralph Carlton Insurance Agency	Wallace, NV	1993
Wall Insurance Agency	Eden, NC	1993
Cummings-LeGrand Insurance Agency	Shelby, NC	1994
Boyette Insurance	Fayetteville, NC	1995
McLean Brady McLean Insurance	Lumberton, NC	1995
Poole Insurance Agency	Greensboro, NC	1995
Webb Insurance	Statesville, NC	1995
Frank Wilson Agency	Rocky Mount, NC	1995
James R. Lingle Agency, Inc.	Florence, SC	1996
William Goldsmith Agency	Greenville, SC	1996
C. Dan Joyner Insurance Agency	Greenville, SC	1996
Boyle-Vaughan Associates	Columbia, SC	1996
Consumers Title Company	Fayetteville, NC	1997
DeJarnette & Paul, Inc.	Richmond, VA	1998
W.C. Brown Insurance Services	Rocky Mount, NC	1998
McPhail, Bray, Murphy & Allen	Charlotte, NC	1998
Cameron Harris & Associates	Morganton, NC	1998
Blue Ridge Burke	Winston-Salem, NC	1999
Huffines-Russell Insurance Agency	Alpharetta, GA	1999
Old Dominion Insurance Services, Inc.	Pulaski, VA	1999
Givens & Williams, Inc.	Fairfax, VA	1999
James River Title Agency, Inc.	Richmond, VA	1999
E. W. Barger & Company	Waynesboro, VA	1999
G. C. Wright Company, Inc.	Petersburg, VA	1999
Beam, Cooper, Gainey and Associates	Morehead City, NC	1999
Pioneer Title / MidAtlantic Title	Virginia Beach, VA	1999
The Kay Company	Lumberton, NC	1999
Ingram-McDaniel Insurance Associates	Thomaston, GA	1999
Macon Insurance Associates	Macon, GA	1999
Piedmont Administrators	Greensboro, NC	2000
Pruden Risk Management	Dalton, GA	2000
Asura Corporation	Research Triangle Park, NC	2000
Chaney Thomas	Roanoke, VA	2000
Poindexter and Associates Inc.	Martinsville, Va	2000
Thornton & Harwell Agency	Brentwood, TN	2000
Clark Consulting Group Inc.	Roanoke, VA	2001
Stephens & Company Insurance Services Inc.	Kennesaw, GA	2001
First American Title of the Carolinas, LLC	Charlotte, NC	2001
Lowery D. Finley and Company	Virginia Beach, VA	2001
Lofton and Company	Savannah, GA	2001
U.S. Insurance Services	Greenville, SC	2001
Cooney Rickard & Curtin Inc.	Birmingham, AL	2001

TABLE XVI
BB&T Insurance Acquisitions *(continued)*

Company	Location	Date
O'Neal & Hinson	Macon, GA	2001
Professional Benefits Management Inc.	Greensboro, NC	2002
Kaplan Insurance, Macon Georgia	Macon, GA	2002
Benefit Consultants of Virginia, Inc.	Richmond, VA	2002
American Marketing Center	NY, NY	2002
Piedmont Brokerage Services LLC	High Point, NC	2002
Landrum-Yaeger & Associates, Inc.	Tallahassee, Fl	2002
Carolina Insurance Consultants, Inc.	Greenville, SC	2002
Cranman & Company Inc.	Savannah, GA	2003
Old Colony Insurance Services, Inc.	Louisville, KY	2003
Cromwell Agency	Lexington, KY	2003
Southern Cross Underwriters	Jackson, MS	2003
STHARCO Inc.	Kingsport, TN	2003
Cooper, Love & Jackson	Nashville, TN	2003
Surety Land Title	Raleigh, NC	2003
McGriff, Seibels & Williams	Birmingham, Al	2004
Iler Wall & Shonter	St. Petersburg, Fl	2004
Allied Insurance Group	Dalton, GA	2004
Employee Benefit Services	Lexington, KY	2004
Universal Specialty Underwriters	Tampa, FL	2004
L.W. Legge Agency, Inc.	Cookville, TN	2004
Lighthouse Title, LLP	Fairfax, VA	2004
Stewart Smith East, Inc.		2004
Langan Insurance, Benefits & Financial Services	Louisville, KY	2004
Huffaker & Trimble Inc.	Chattanooga, TN	2005
Tom Bennett / Palmer & Cay (Book of Business)	Norcross, GA	2005
Sterling West Insurance Services, Inc.	Glendale, CA	2005
Swett & Crawford of Texas, Inc. (Book of Business)	Houston, TX	2005
Ronald Luke & Associates, Inc.	Houston, TX	2005
VISTA Insurance Partners, Inc.	San Antonio, TX	2005
Negley Associates, inc	Cedar Grove, NJ	2005
Wyman, Green & Blalock	Bradenton, FL	2006
Reese Insurance Associates, Inc.	Riverdale, GA	2007
Carswell Insurance Services	Hilton Head, SC	2007
Sidney O. Smith Inc.	Alpharetta, GA	2007
Heritage Title Services of Louisville, Ky	Louisville, KY	2007
Ott & Company	Alpharetta, GA	2008
Ramsay Title Group	Norcross, GA	2008
Burkey Risk Services	Maitland, FL	2008
Savannah Reinsurance Underwriting Management LLC	Stamford, CT	2008
Premier Benefits Group	Alpharetta, GA	2008
Union Bank Insurance Services, Inc.	San Diego, CA	2008
Puckett, Scheetz & Hogan	Myrtle Beach, SC	2008
Southern Risk Holdings, Inc.	Sumter, SC	2008
Commercial Title Group	Vienna, VA	2008
J. Rolfe Davis Insurance Agency Inc.	Maitland, FL	2008
TapCo Underwriters, Inc.	Burlington, NC	2008
Oswald Trippe and Co. Inc.	Ft. Myers, FL	2009
Liberty Benefit Insurance Services	San Jose, CA	2011
Atlantic Risk Management Corporation	Columbia, MD	2011
F.B.P. Insurance Services, LLC (Precept Advisory Group, LLC)	Irvine, CA	2011

TABLE XVII
BB&T Non-Bank Acquisitions

Company	*Location*	*Date*
Interstate Leasing Services	Charlotte, NC	1974
Marvin Greene Mortgage Company	Charlotte, NC	1974
Nexus	Raleigh, NC	1992
Farr	Greensboro, NC	1994
Goddard Technology	Greenville, SC	1994
Leasing Associates Inc.	Greenville, SC	1994
Prime Rate Premium Finance	Florence, SC	1994
Autobase	Charlotte, NC	1996
Regional Acceptance	Greenville, NC	1996
Craigie	Richmond, VA	1997
Phillips Factors	High Point, NC	1997
Sheffield/Refloat	Clemmons, ND	1997
Dealers Credit Incorporated	Menomonee Falls, WI	1998
W.E. Stanley	Greensboro, NC	1998
Scott & Stringfellow	Richmond, VA	1999
Laureate Capital Corp.	Charlotte, NC	2000
Edgar Norris	Greenville,NC	2000
The Southeastern Trust Company	Greenville, SC	2001
Horizon Mortgage Company	Atlanta, GA	2001
Ryan Lee	McLean, VA	2002
Virginia Investment Counselors	Norfolk, VA	2002
The Pfefferkorn Company	Winston-Salem, NC	2002
Hunt Dupree Rhine & Associates	Greenville, SC	2002
Southeast Fidelity Corporation	Tallahassee, Fl	2002
Capital Premium Plan	Charlotte, NC	2004
deGarmo & Kelleher	Washington, DC	2004
U.S. Bancorp Consumer Finance of Kentucky	Paducah, Ky	2004
Windsor Entities	Reston, VA	2005
Sterling Capital Management LLC	Charlotte, NC	2005
R. J. Twitty & Company	Tampa, FL	2005
Wilson & Nolan Southeast Inc	Atlanta, Ga	2005
Bergen Capital Incorporated	Hasbrouck, NJ	2005
FSB Financial, Inc.	Arlington, TX	2006
AFCO Credit Corporation/CAFO, Inc.	NY, NY/Ontario, Canada	2006
Collateral Real Estate Capital, LLC	Birmingham, AL	2007
Live Oak Capital Ltd.	Houston, TX	2008
Cananwill, Inc.	Philadelphia, PA	2009
BFG Realty Advisors, LLC	Louisville, KY	2009
Quantum First Capital, LTD	Dallas, TX	2009

The Romantic Diary
of a Stock Certificate

July 1921. I am Stock Certificate number 777 for five shares of the $100 par stock of Branch Banking and Trust Company. I was transferred today to a new owner. A young businesswoman bought me for $200 per share – an investment of $1,000. I am currently paying quarterly dividends of 3 percent. I hope she is pleased with the returns I bring her.

December 1923. I have paid my new owner a 3-percent dividend each quarter for the past two and a half years.

December 1926. For the last three years I have added a 4-percent special dividend to the regular 3-percent quarterly dividends, giving my owner an annual return of $80.

April 1931. The special dividend went to 8 percent in December 1928, over and above the regular 3-percent quarterly. It has remained at that figure for three consecutive years – a yield of 10 percent, or $100 per year on my owner's investment. I paid my regular quarterly 3-percent for the first two quarters this year; but something big is afoot! This month I am issuing a 60-percent stock dividend; so from now on, her ownership will be a total of eight shares instead of the original five.

December 1931. For the last two quarters of this year I paid 2 percent per annum on eight shares, which was a small gain over the 3-percent on five that I paid before. Remember, this is a depression year. Many banks have failed during 1931.

December 1932. I paid a straight 2-percent quarterly dividend - $64. Not bad in these hard times.

December 1934. In spite of a bank holiday and other disturbances in the economic world, I maintained my 2-percent quarterly payments until the last quarter of 1934 – when it seemed best to reduce them to $1.90 – but I came across with $63.20 per annum on eight shares, so I don't think I need to apologize!

December 1935. I paid $2 per share each quarter and a $2 special this year - $80 on my owner's investment.

December 1942. For the past seven years I have paid $2 per share every quarter and at every year-end I paid a $4 special, a total of $96 per annum.

December 1945. Since 1943 I have been paying a $7 special dividend each December and regular $2 quarterly dividends: $120 per year.

December 1946. I began paying a $3 quarterly dividend this year, and a mid-year $5 special, plus an $8 special at year-end. This brought my owner an income of $200 this year.

October 1948. I paid a $3 quarterly dividend on the $100 par stock the first of each quarter; and on the fifth of this month those shares were split into $25 par and a 25-percent stock dividend paid in addition. Thus my owner received 32 of the new shares in exchange for her eight old ones, and a bonus of eight shares, so she now owns 40 shares.

December 1948. I paid a special cash dividend of $1.60 on the new $25 par shares, a total of $160 in addition to the 25-percent stock dividend.

December 1949. My new dividend rate on the $25 par shares was set at $0.75, which was paid each quarter this year, plus a special of $3 per share, providing my owner a $240 annual return on her investment.

December 1951. Things get better! This year I paid $1 per quarter and a special of $4 per share in December.

February 1953. I paid a 100-percent stock dividend this month! Now my owner has 80 shares of $25 par stock.

January 1957. Each of my $25 par shares split into five $5 par shares, giving my owner 400 shares instead of 80.

December 1957. The new $5 par shares paid a quarterly dividend of $0.25 and a special of $0.50: $1.50 per share on 400 – a new high of $600. After payment of the special on Dec. 15, I also paid another 100-percent stock dividend; so my owner now has 800 shares of $5 par stock.

December 1960. I paid $0.15 per quarter for the first three quarters this year, but I stepped it up a nickel per share for the fourth quarter. That nickel made a difference of $40 on my owner's 800 shares; and I paid a $0.40 special this month, so the original $1,000 produced $840 income this year.

October 1963. To date I have paid my owner total cash dividends of $11,504.40 and have never missed a single quarterly payment. The five shares of $100 par stock she purchased in 1921 have become 800 shares of $5 par stock; the $1,000 investment now represents a worth of $58,800, as the last sale of stock on Sept. 20, 1963, brought $73.50 per share. In 1962 the annual dividends paid reached $1,000, equaling for the first time her total original investment in the five shares of stock.

June 1967. After paying $0.40 for the first two quarters, I paid another 100-percent stock dividend, which increased my owner's number of shares to 1,600.

July 1974. A big change occurred this month! BB&T shareholders traded their $5 par value stock for two shares of $2.50 par value stock in the newly formed Branch Corporation, a one-bank holding company. This means that my owner now has 3,200 shares.

January 1979. A 10-percent stock dividend brought my owner's number of shares to 3,520.

October 1979. A second 10-percent stock dividend was declared this year, bringing my total to 3,872 shares. My owner has left me to her daughter. I can now help her reach her financial goals.

December 1987. A 100-percent stock dividend was declared this month, which means my owner now holds 7,744 shares.

December 1991. During the past four years, I have paid a total of $23,928.96 in dividends.

December 1995. My number of shares skyrocket after BB&T Financial Corporation and Southern National Corporation are combined in a merger of equals. My owner now has 11,229 shares, thanks to the 1.45 shares of Southern National Corporation she received in exchange for each share of BB&T Financial Corporation. My dividend checks brought in $11,228.80 to my owner this year. She now watches my progress on the New York Stock Exchange where I am traded under the symbol "SNB".

June 1997. I can hardly believe it. The stock price has tripled since the merger of equals was announced in August 1994 and more than doubled in the past year. Last month, we were renamed BB&T Corporation and our trading symbol changed to "BBK" on the New York Stock Exchange.

December 1997. BB&T was added to the S&P 500 index on Dec. 3. My price per share surged to close that day at $65.

August 1998. My price increased to $70.62 and BB&T declared a 2-for-1 stock split so now my owner has 22,458 shares. I pay a dividend of $0.175 per share, which makes my owner $3,930.15 quarterly.

January 1999. I am now traded on the New York Stock Exchange under the trading symbol of "BBT".

December 2002. During this year my quarterly cash dividend was increased by 11.5 percent, making 2002 the 31st consecutive year BB&T has increased its dividend. I have paid a dividend every year since 1903.

December 2004. I am proud to be an investment in the ninth largest banking organization in the United States with consolidated assets totaling $100.5 billion as of Dec. 31, 2004.

August 2007. BB&T Corporation has been steadily growing and my dividend has increased every year. I currently pay $0.46 per share to my owner.

August 2009. Due to deteriorating economic conditions, the very difficult decision was made to reduce my dividend to $0.15. I am proud that BB&T was the last large bank to reduce our dividend, and I still pay a premium compared to all other large banks.

March 2011. My new owner, the grandson of my original owner, was happy to hear that my dividend was increased to $0.16 and that there would be an additional one-time $0.01 dividend paid second quarter. BB&T was the first large bank to announce an increase in its dividend.

May 2011. As of the close of the market on May 31, 2011, I was worth $618,493.32, not bad for a $1,000 investment.

Bibliography

BOOKS

Ashe, Samuel A'Court, *History of North Carolina* From 1783 to 1925, Vol. II, Edwards and Broughton, Raleigh, 1925.

Bassett, John Spencer, *A Short History of the United States*, Fifth edition, The McMillan Company, New York, 1943.

Benton, Elbert J., *A Century of Progress*, The National City Bank of Cleveland, Cleveland, 1945.

Connor, R. D. W., *Biographical History of North Carolina*, Vol. IV, Edited by Samuel A'Court Ashe, Published by Charles L. Van Noppen, Greensboro, 1906.

—, *North Carolina: Rebuilding an Ancient Commonwealth*, 1584-1925, Vol. III, The American Historical Society, Inc., New York, 1929.

Cross, Marion E., *Pioneer Harvest*, The Farmers and Mechanics Savings Bank of Minneapolis, Minneapolis, 1949.

Daniels, Josephus, *Tar Heel Editor*, The University of North Carolina Press, Chapel Hill, 1939.

Hamilton, J. G. deRoulhac, *History of North Carolina*, The Lewis Publishing Company, Chicago, 1919.

Henderson, Archibald, *North Carolina, The Old North State and The New*, Vol. II, The Lewis Publishing Company, Chicago, 1941.

History of North Carolina, Vols. IV, V, The Lewis Publishing Company, Chicago, 1919

Hobbs, Samuel H., Jr., *North Carolina: An Economic and Social Profile*, The University of North Carolina Press, Chapel Hill, 1958. —, North Carolina: Economic and Social, The University of North Carolina Press, Chapel Hill, 1930.

Holdsworth, John Thom, *Money and Banking*, Sixth edition, D. Appleton-Century Company, Inc., New York and London, 1937.

Johnson, Clint, *Service None Better: The History of Southern National Bank*, Corporate Stories, Atlanta, 1997.

Lawrence, Robert C., *Here in Carolina*, J. J. Little and Ives Company, New York, 1939.

Moore, John W., *School History of North Carolina*, Alfred Williams and Company, Raleigh, 1886.

The National Cyclopaedia of American Biography, Vol. IV, James T. White and Company, New York, 1893.

North Carolina, Vol. III, The American Historical Society, Inc., Chicago and New York, 1928.

North Carolina Business Directory, Edited by Rev. L. Branson, Published by J. A. Jones, Raleigh, 1872.

North Carolina History Told by Contemporaries, Edited by Hugh Talmage Lefler, The University of North Carolina Press, 1934.

The North Carolina Yearbook, Published by the News and Observer, Raleigh, 1922.

Wilson Chamber of Commerce, *Wilson North Carolina: A Pictorial History*, Wilson Chamber of Commerce, Wilson, 1993.

GOVERNMENT PUBLICATIONS

The Executive Documents. Printed by Order of the House of Representatives During the Second Session of the 42nd Congress. Government Printing Office. Washington, D.C., 1872.

Reports of the Condition of the State, Private and Savings Banks at the Close of Business November 27, 1908. Department of the North Carolina Corporation Commission, Raleigh, 1908.

U.S. Bureau of the Census, *U.S. Census of Population: 1960. Number of Inhabitants, North Carolina*, Final Report PC (1)-35A. U. S. Government Printing Office, Washington, D.C. 1961.

NEWSPAPERS AND PERIODICALS

Daily Times, Wilson, N.C. Sept. 9, 1903; July 26, 1921; Aug. 21, 1927; Oct. 30, 1929; Jan. 7, 1932; Mar. 9, 1933; Mar. 10, 1933; Mar. 14, 1933.

Gardner, O. Max, "One State Cleans House." *Saturday Evening Post*, January 2, 1932.

"His Banking Policies Have Been Tried and Have Met Every Test Against Them." *The State Magazine*, Vol. 1, No. 18. Sept. 30, 1933.

Maxwell, A. J., "Economic Progress in North Carolina Since 1900." *News Letter*. Vol. XXXII, No. 5, The University of North Carolina, Chapel Hill, March 13, 1946.

News and Observer, Raleigh, June 5, 1896; Nov. 5, 1907.

"North Carolina's Trust Development." *Tarheel Banker*, Vol. IV, No. 10, April, 1926.

Wilson *Advance*, February 2, 1893.

Wilson Daily Times, Jan. 10, 1950; Centennial issue, 1955; March 1, 1962.

Wilson *Mirror*, Sept. 10, 1890; Jan. 10, 1893.

Wilson *Times*, Sept. 4, 1896; Dec. 25, 1903; Nov. 20, 1908; Aug. 16, 1912; Dec. 20, 1912; Apr. 30, 1915; Aug. 30, 1915; Nov. 26, 1915; Dec. 17, 1915; Mar. 23, 1920.

Zion's Landmark, Wilson, N. C., Nov. 15, 1886.

"Dream Team" *Triad Business Journal*, Greensboro, N.C., Vol. 4, No. 23, Feb. 1-7, 2002

UNPUBLISHED WORKS

Mitchell, Herbert Hall, *The Development of Commercial Banking in North Carolina, 1865-1935,* Unpublished Ph.D. dissertation, University of North Carolina, Chapel Hill, 1954.

INTERVIEWS

Henry Groves Connor III, attorney, Wilson, N. C., March 14, 1962. Grandson of former president.

Mrs. Margaret Connor Simpson, Raleigh, N. C., March 12, 1962. Daughter of a former president and daughter-in-law of a former president.

C. C. Ware, Wilson, N. C., January 17, 1962, and subsequent interviews. Historian and archivist.

Mrs. P. L. Woodard, Wilson, N. C., April 4, 1962. Widow of former director. Only Wilsonian who has personally known every president.

Thomas Hadley Woodard, Wilson, N. C., March 16, 1962. Grandson of Thomas Hadley.

Interviews with officers of the bank during February, March and April 1962:
Frederick Louis Carr, chairman of the board. Grandson of Alpheus Branch.
Joshua Ernest Paschall, president.
S. S. Lawrence, executive vice president.
John A. Campbell, Jr., executive vice president.
E. B. Crow, senior vice president and senior trust officer.
J. L. Satchwell, senior vice president and cashier.
H. S. Bateman, vice president. Son of former president.

Interviews during September, October and November 2011:
Kelly S. King, chairman and chief executive officer
John A. Allison, former chairman and chief executive officer
Chris L. Henson, chief operating officer
Daryl N. Bible, chief financial officer and senior executive vice president
Clarke R. Starnes, chief risk officer and senior executive vice president
Steve B. Wiggs, chief marketing officer and senior executive vice president
Ricky K. Brown, president, community banking and senior executive vice president
Henry Williamson, former chief operating officer and senior executive vice president
Ken Chalk, former chief credit officer and senior executive vice president
Scott Reed, former chief financial officer and senior executive vice president
Leon Wilson, operations manager and senior executive vice president
Barbara F. Duck, enterprise risk manager and senior executive vice president
Donna Goodrich, deposit services manager and senior executive vice president
James Maynard, former director of BB&T Corporation Board
Alan Greer, director of Investor Relations

CORRESPONDENCE

Sons of J. C. Hales:
C. S. Hales, St. Petersburg, Florida. Letter dated March 6, 1962.
Felix S. Hales, Cleveland, Ohio. Letter dated March 7, 1962.
Raleigh S. Hales, Pasadena, California. Letter dated April 4, 1962.

ADDITIONAL SOURCES

Bullock, James Dempsey, *Early Wilson*, Unpublished manuscript. State Library. No date.

Groven, Cleo, *One Hundred Years of Progress*, The Piqua National Bank and Trust Company, Piqua, Ohio, 1947.

Highlights of 75 Years in Mobile, The First National Bank of Mobile, Mobile, Alabama, 1940.

McGill, Ralph, *Story of the Trust Company of Georgia*, The Trust Company of Georgia, Atlanta, 1951.

North, Edgerton G., *The First Hundred Years*, The Williamsburgh Savings Bank, Brooklyn, 1951.

Quigley, Martin, *St. Louis, A Fond Look Back*, The First National Bank in St. Louis, St. Louis, 1956.

Riebel, R. C., *Louisville Panorama*, Second edition, Liberty National Bank and Trust Company, Louisville, Kentucky, 1954.

Tymeson, Mildred McClary, *Worcester Bankbook*, Worcester County Trust Company, Worcester, 1955.

Williams, Frances Leigh, *They Faced the Future*, State-Planters Bank and Trust Company, 1951.

1784-1934, The First National Bank of Boston, The First National Bank of Boston, Boston, 1934.

75 Years of Banking, Mellon National Bank, 1944.

Footnotes

CHAPTER II

1   R. D. W. Connor, *North Carolina: Rebuilding an Ancient Commonwealth*, Vol. III, The American Historical Society, Inc., New York, 1929, p. 1011.

2   J. G. deRoulhac Hamilton, *History of North Carolina*, Vol. III, The Lewis Publishing Company, Chicago, 1919, pp. 161-162.

3   Samuel A'Court Ashe, *History of North Carolina from 1783 to 1925*, Vol. II, Edwards and Broughton, Raleigh, 1925, p. 1144.

4   Herbert Hall Mitchell, *The Development of Commercial Banking in North Carolina*, 1865-1935, unpublished Ph.D. dissertation, University of North Carolina, Chapel Hill, 1954, pp. 47-48.

5   Ashe, p. 1144.

6   Mitchell, pp. 21-22.

7   Mitchell, p. 32.

8   Connor, pp. 312-314.

9   John W. Moore, *School History of North Carolina*, Alfred Williams and Company, Raleigh, 1886, p. 27.

10   Hugh Talmage Lefler, *North Carolina History Told by Contemporaries*, The University of North Carolina Press, Chapel Hill, 1934, p. 364.

11   *Ibid*, p. 372.

12   *Ibid*.

13   Mitchell, p. 166.

14   Sources: Herbert Hall Mitchell, *op.cit.*; *The Executive Documents Printed by Order of the House of Representatives during the Second Session of the Forty Second Congress*, Government Printing Office, 1872; *The North Carolina Yearbook*, published by the *News and Observer*, Raleigh, 1922; *North Carolina Business Directory*, ed. by Rev. L. Branson, published by J. A. Jones, Raleigh, 1872; various city directories.

CHAPTER III

1   Archibald Henderson, North Carolina, *The Old North State and The New*, Vol. II, Lewis Publishing Company, Chicago, 1941, p. 341.

2   Herbert Hall Mitchell, *op.cit.*, p. 167.

3   *The National Cyclopaedia of American Biography*, Vol. IV, James T. White and Company, New York, 1893, p. 237.

4   *Wilson Daily Times*, Wilson, N. C., January 10, 1950, p. 10.

5   Daybook, Branch and Company, p. 8.

6   *National Cyclopaedia*, p. 237.

7   *Daily Times*, Wilson, N.C., August 21, 1927.

8   R.D.W. Connor, *Biographical History of North Carolina*, edited by Samuel A. Ashe, Vol. 4, published by Charles L. Van Noppen, Greensboro, N. C., 1906, p. 152.

9   John Spencer Bassett, *A Short History of the United States*, fifth edition, The MacMillan Company, New York, 1943, pp. 664-665.

10   Samuel H. Hobbs, Jr., *North Carolina: Economic and Social*, Chapel Hill, The University of North Carolina Press, 1930, p. 151.

11   Located at State Department of Archives, Raleigh, in ledger entitled, "List of State Treasurer's Accounts with Various Banks, 1871–1876," Vol. 30, p. 34.

12   *Zion's Landmark*, P. D. Gold Publishing Company, Wilson, N. C., November 15, 1886.

13   Josephus Daniels, *Tar Heel Editor*, The University of North Carolina Press, Chapel Hill, 1939, p. 150.
14   *ibid*, p. 150.
15   *ibid*, p. 152.
16   Articles of Incorporation and By-Laws, Branch Banking and Trust Company, pp. iii, iv.
17   Mitchell, pp. 76, 78.
18   Wilson *Mirror*, September 10, 1890, p. 4.
19   Daniels, *op.cit.*, p. 152.
20   Henderson, *op.cit.*, p. 376.
21   *Wilson Daily Times*, Sec. C, 1955.
22   Will of Alpheus Branch recorded in Wilson County Courthouse, Item VIII.
23   Cross, *op.cit.*, p. 109.
24   Mitchell, p. 177.
25   Hobbs, *op.cit.*, p. 151.
26   Wilson *Mirror*, January 10, 1893.
27   W. P. Simpson, letter to Jas. G. Mehegan Esq., cashier in Tarboro, July 13, 1895, found in bank records of the time.
28   Minutes, North Carolina Bankers Association, Raleigh.
29   Correspondence, North Carolina Bankers Association, Raleigh.

CHAPTER VI

1   Vernon Morton, *Wilson Daily Times*, January 10, 1950, p. 5.
2   *Daily Times*, Wilson, N. C., September 9, 1903, p. 4.
3   Minutes, Branch Banking and Trust Company, 1903-1910, pp. 31, 32, 34.
4   Robert C. Lawrence, *Here in Carolina*, J. J. Little and Ives Company, New York, 1939, pp. 52-54.
5   Wilson *Times*, March 23, 1920, p. 1.
6   Hugh Talmage Lefler, p. 403.
7   Herbert Hall Mitchell, op.cit., p. 224.
8   Mitchell, op.cit., p. 232.
9   "North Carolina's Trust Development," *Tarheel Banker*, April 1926, p. 41.
10   *Reports of the Condition of the State, Private and Savings Banks at the Close of Business November 27, 1908*, Department of the North Carolina Corporation Commission, Raleigh, 1908, p. 118.
11   John Thom Holdsworth, *Money and Banking*, sixth edition, D. Appleton-Century Company, Inc., New York and London, 1937, pp. 265-266.
12   Raleigh News and Observer, November 5, 1907, p. 1.
13   Minutes, 1903-1910, p. 48.
14   Minutes, 1903-1910, p. 49.
15   *Ibid*.
16   Minutes, 1903-1910, p. 62.
17   Minutes, 1903-1910, p. 64.
18   Minutes, 1910-1912, p. 42.
19   Minutes, 1910-1912, p. 44.
20   *Ibid*.

CHAPTER VII

1   John Thom Holdsworth, *op.cit.*, p. 258.
2   Holdsworth, p. 505.
3   Elbert J. Benton, *A Century of Progress*, The National City Bank of Cleveland, Cleveland, 1945, pp. 30-31.
4   Holdsworth, p. 506.
5   Minutes, Branch Banking and Trust Company, 1914-1916, pp. 50-51.

6   Minutes, 1914-1916, p. 45.
7   Minutes, 1914-1916, p. 47.
8   Minutes, 1914-1916, p. 54.
9   Minutes, 1917-1925, pp. 21-22
10   Minutes, 1917-1925, p. 23.
11   Benton, pp. 21-22.
12   Samuel H. Hobbs, Jr., *op.cit.*, p. 170.
13   Herbert Hall Mitchell, *op.cit.*, p. 238.
14   *Daily Times*, Wilson, N. C., July 26, 1921.
15   Sources: Various records in the office of the North Carolina State Banking
     Commission, Raleigh.
16   Mitchell, *op.cit.*, p. 117.
17   Minutes, pp. 107, 123, 148.
18   Benton, *op.cit.*, pp. 35-37.
19   *Ibid.*
20   Minutes, 1917-1925, p. 113.
21   Minutes, 1917-1925, p. 173.
22   Minutes, Branch Investment Company. p. 31.
23   O. Max Gardner, "One State Cleans House," *Saturday Evening Post*, January 2,
     1932, p. 72.
24   *Daily Times*. Wilson, N. C., October 30, 1929, p. 8.
25   *Ibid.*, p. 4.
26   *Daily Times*, January 7, 1932, p. 4.
27   Minutes, 1925-1932, p. 173.
28   Marion. E. Cross. *op.cit.*, pp. 32-33.
29   *Daily Times*, March 14, 1933, p. 4.
30   *Daily Times*, March 10, 1933, p. 4.
31   *Daily Times*, March 9, 1933, p. 4.
32   Sources: Mitchell, pp. 392, 388.

CHAPTER VIII

1   John Thom Holdsworth, *op.cit.*, p. 221.
2   Minutes, Branch Banking and Trust Company, 1932-1939, pp. 35-38.
3   Holdsworth, *op.cit.*,p. 91.
4   Holdsworth, *Ibid*, p. 261.
5   Herbert Hall Mitchell, *op.cit.*, p. 425.
6   A. J. Maxwell, "Economic Progress in North Carolina Since 1900," University of North
     Carolina *News Letter*, Vol. XXXII, No. 5, March 13, 1946.
7   Mitchell, *op.cit.*, pp. 427-428.
8   Minutes, 1939-1944, p. 146.
9   Minutes, 1949-1951, p. 239.

CHAPTER IX

1   U.S. Bureau of the Census, *U.S. Census of Population: 1960. Number of
     Inhabitants, North Carolina*, Final Report PC (1)-35A. U.S. Government Printing
     Office, Washington, D.C., 1961, pp. 13-14.
2   Minutes, 1956-1957, p. 187.
3   Minutes, February 24, 1970.
4   William S. Gray, Senior Vice President, Harris Trust and Savings Bank, Chicago,
     Illinois, speech entitled, "Long-Term Outlook of the U.S. Economy and Stock Market,"
     10th Congress of the European Federation of Financial Analysts Societies, Brussels,
     Belgium, October 8-11, 1978.
5   *Ibid.*

6   *Handbook of Securities of the United States Government and Federal Agencies,*
     First Boston, New York, New York, 1976, p. 7.
7   *Handbook of Securities of the United States Government and Federal Agencies,*
     op.cit., p. 9.
8   Herbert E. Neil, Jr., Vice President and Economist, Hams Trust and Savings Bank,
     Chicago, Illinois, speech entitled, "Capital Spending Outlook with an Impending
     Recession," 24th Annual Convention of the Material Handling Equipment Distribution
     Association, Doral Country Club, Miami, Florida, May 1, 1979.
9   Minutes, March 20, 1973.

CHAPTER X

1   Interviews with Harllee W. Lyon, Senior Vice President, Investments/Funds
     Management Department on January 16, 1986.
2   Source: *Wall Street Journal,* New York, New York, October 20, 1987, 1. c.
3   Minutes, April 19, 1983.

BIOGRAPHIES

1   Sources: *Wilson Advance.* Wilson, N. C.: February 2, 1893: History of North Carolina.
     Chicago and New York: The Lewis Publishing Company, 1919, Vol. IV, pp. 129-130;
     The National Cyclopaedia of American Biography, New York: James T. White and
     Company, 1893, Vol. IV. pp. 237-238.
2   Source: Interview with Mrs. P. L. Woodard on April 4, 1962.
3   Sources: *North Carolina.* Chicago and New York: The American Historical Society,
     Inc., 1928, Vol. III. p. 497; Robert C. Lawrence, Here in Carolina. New York: J. J. Little
     & Ives Company. 1939, pp. 52-53; and interviews with his daughter, Mrs. Margaret
     Connor Simpson on March 12, 1962, and grandson, H. G. Connor III, on March 14,
     1962.
4   Sources: Wilson *Daily Times,* January 10, 1950; Correspondence with his sons:
     C. S. Hales, March 6, 1962; Felix S. Hales, March 7, 1962; Raleigh S. Hales, April 4,
     1962.
5   Source: Wilson *Daily Times,* March 1, 1962.
6   Sources: *History of North Carolina,* Chicago and New York: Lewis Publishing
     Company, 1919, Vol. V, p. 135: Archibald Henderson, North Carolina, *The Old North
     State and the New,* Chicago: Lewis Publishing Company, 1941, Vol. III, pp. 187-188.
7   Source: Interview with H. S. Bateman, son of H. D. Bateman, on March 15, 1962.
8   Source: Interview with Mr. Paschall on March 1, 1962 and with General James
     Paschall on November 25, 1985.
9   Source: Interview with Mr. Carr on March 24, 1962 and August 21, 1979 and with
     Olivia Stuart on November 26, 1985.
10   Source: Interview with Mr. Satchwell on September 27, 1979.
11   Source: Interview with Mr. Gregory on September 25, 1979 and with Mrs. Gregory on
     December 30, 1985.
12   Source: Interview with Mr. Tucker on April 20, 1990.
13   Source: Various records in the office of the State Banking Commission, Raleigh, N.C.
     and corporate minutes.
14   Compiled with assistance of Gail Flowers and Caroline Canady, 1997.